Do

Dominic Óg agus Niamh

Faoí Ghlas

le Dominic Adams

Faoi Ghlas testimonials.

"I sat down intending to only read a few pages but finished the book in one go. It's a great read, everyone should get a copy."

Paul Maskey. MP for West Belfast.

"Faoi Ghlas brought back memories. It made me laugh and cry but it also brought back that anger of how we all lived and how we learned to cope, and of course, how brave the women were."

Bernadette Maguire. Daughter of a former Republican prisoner.

This is the second edition of Faoi Ghlas. The first was released in November 2010. There are some slight additions but not enough to alter the shape of the story in any huge way. At the suggestion of Joe McCormack and Chris Hughes, I have included a glossary which may help in the understanding of the jail slang which was second nature to prisoners.

Since 2010 two people who I thought a lot of have departed this world for the next.

Alfie Hannaway was my cousin but he was much more than that. A huge friend to me, my mentor; I loved him and if I had to choose any man to have been my father it would have been Alfie.

My Aunt Rita Adams was a Falls Road woman but spent most of her life in Canada. She never forgot her Irish roots and never forgot her imprisoned relatives in Ireland. She was also a great Máthair Mór to my children.

An awful lot of Republican ex-prisoners have died since 2010 including some mentioned in the first edition of Faoi Ghlas. Bíonn said inár smaointe I gconaí.

Mar a thug mé buiochais do Irene i 2010 tugaim buiochais arís dí.

The same to Gerry and Padraig for their encouragement and guidance; and of course Dominic Óg agus Niamh for the planting of the seed agus ár dha madadh, Fionn agus Simba.

Dominic Adams

July 2016

©2016 Dominic Adams

Alfie Hannaway (middle) with ex prisoner Paul Rooney (left and the author (right) standing at the entrance to the Long Kesh site 2005.

Máthair Mór. Aunt Rita Adams pictured at her home in Toronto in 2009. Despite being so far away, she never forgot her roots.

Dominic and Niamh on a visit to the Blocks 2005

Dominic and Dominic Óg at the Bobby Sands Commemoration
May 2015

Foreword

Dominic Adams was six years old in 1971 when he first experienced life in Long Kesh.

He was brought there on a visit to his oldest brother Gerry who was interned at the time.

Long Kesh has played a huge part in his and his family's life over the last forty years - four of his brothers were imprisoned there and three of his brothers-in-law also spent time in Long Kesh.

Many of his friends ended up in the prison as the war impacted on the community of Ballymurphy where Dominic was born and grew up.

Now a father of two children, Dominic Óg and Niamh, Dominic returned to the prison in 2005 with his children to show them where their father spent the formative years of his life as a political prisoner.

Today, Long Kesh is a listed site where political ex-prisoners, their families and those interested can visit the jail and experience what thousands of political prisoners lived through, some for decades.

They can also visit the prison hospital (also a listed building) where in 1981, ten republican prisoners died on hunger strike.

Preserving Long Kesh in bricks and mortar is a significant and permanent monument to both a heroic and tragic part of Ireland's long struggle for independence and unity.

People can visit it and allow all of their senses especially their eyes and ears to experience life in one of the world's most infamous detention centres.

In the introduction to his book Faoi Ghlas, Dominic Adams describes being motivated to write this jail memoir by 'the many questions asked of me by my two children' and by a belief that 'every ex-prisoner should record their memoirs, either written or orally'

Dominic, in words, is doing what those involved in maintaining the site at Long Kesh are doing - preserving the past for future generations.

In this light hearted and easily read account of seven years in prison in both the Crum and the H-Blocks of Long Kesh between 1984 and 1991 Dominic records a different and more relaxed phase in the life of republican political prisoners and the prison's life.

And as someone who has been to jail three times I use the word 'relaxed' with a huge health warning because being in jail is not a good experience no matter the conditions.

While there you make the best of it while at all times waiting for the day when the gates fly open.

But by the time Dominic arrived behind bars the protest for political status in the H-Blocks and Armagh Women's Prison and the deaths of the hunger strikers had won not only political status but prison conditions which allowed the prisoners to serve their time free from intimidation and harassment by prison warders.

Active republicans, once recruited, were warned sternly and with a sense of gallows humour that there were two certainties: jail or death.

In this book, we are reminded how swiftly jail can arrive into your life and disrupt it dramatically for evermore. No matter how long spent behind bars you never quite kick the jail dust of your shoes, although the longer there the more difficult it is to readjust to life on the outside.

One moment, as in Dominic's case, he and his two comrades are on a mission on Belfast's Ormeau Road and the next moment they are in the custody of the RUC, then charged and then dropped into Belfast's Crumlin Road Jail.

Those who experience it will get a disturbing reminder of 'peering out the small slit that served as a window' as Dominic 'stole a fleeting glance at daily life in Belfast city centre' as he travelled in the back of a prison van or 'meat wagon' as it was known to prisoners.

Through 'small slits' in windows or prison bars is how prisoners view life once they step over the threshold of a prison gate until they are released.

Dominic's immediate experiences on arrival at Crumlin Road jail will jerk the memory of political ex-prisoners and bring them back to this strange world of hostile and aggressive warders, prison numbers, not names, dank smelling cells, the sounds of keys, lock shooting bolts, the stench of hundreds of men 'slopping out' and nerves on edge as the new prisoner tries to defend himself and his integrity as a political not criminal prisoner and the struggle of which he is a part.

Dominic's description of his first visit with his mother and brother Paddy -both veterans of prison life - Annie his mum, from a mother's view point outside the walls and Paddy from inside several jails is emotional.

"My ma had a brave face on her but I knew that beneath the smile, her heart was breaking. I was sorry for the heartache I was bringing her. She was almost sixty years old......'

Annie Adams was there at the beginning of Dominic's seven years in jail and was there at the end as he walked to freedom from the H-Blocks of

Long Kesh, "On the other side of the fence was my mother. "Welcome home son" she said.

Mother's and wives especially, bore the burden of an imprisoned son, daughter, husband or wife. They had to be strong enough to cope with the emotional impact on them, their children and their loved one inside.

Prison life produces dilemmas, too many to mention, all of a challenging nature for the prisoner and Dominic records one in particular for himself while in Crumlin Road jail.

A few months before his arrest, his brother Gerry and a number of other republicans travelling with him in a car in Belfast city centre were shot by a group of loyalists who were arrested at the scene of the shooting.

Two of those loyalists were in a cell yards away from Dominic's cell. He not only had to adjust his psyche to sharing a small piece of space on a landing with loyalist prisoners he also had to manage every day seeing those who tried to kill his brother.

It could not have been easy.

Prison life is made more bearable by those you meet on the inside. It is different from life on the outside as day is to night but is similar to it in terms of those you allow to get close to you or become your friend.

On the outside you will have friends who will make you laugh, cry, guide you, stimulate your mind and relax you.

So too on the inside but in a much more concentrated way and of all the emotions that really helps the time to pass is humour.

And in this booklet it is the 'mixes' which provide the high points which break through the boredom and monotony of prison life.

And the biggest mixers of all in my time in jail and they were still there in Dominic's time were Martin Meehan, Terry 'Cleaky' Clarke, John 'Duice' McMullan; all Belfast men all passed away, who spent decades in jail and who made time that bit easier by making everyone laugh.

As prisoners do, Dominic's time in the H-Blocks was filled out by reading books, learning to speak the Irish language and keeping fit.

It is important to keep busy in prison, to preoccupy your mind to, fill out your day, your week, your year preparing yourself to return to your family and friends.

But it is a tough place and as Dominic reminds us not everyone got through their time unscathed. Some suffered nervous breakdowns due to the stress, anguish and brutality they experienced.

Some carry those scars around with them today and are being helped by organisations like the 'Still Imprisoned' project and the many political ex-prisoner organisations.

In writing this jail journal Dominic Adams is following a well trodden path which stretches back to the middle of the nineteenth century when Fenians like O'Donovan Rossa were imprisoned and later wrote about their experiences.

He has done a service to this recorded history of life behind bars and to the curiosity of his children who will know their father a bit better when they read his journal.

Jim Gibney, October 2010

The idea of recording these memories of my time imprisoned arose from the many questions asked of me by my two children, Dominic Óg and Niamh.

The 25th Anniversary commemorations of the 1981 Hunger Strike and Blanket protests had ignited their curiosity regarding my time in jail and thus I began compiling little incidents and anecdotes that formed my stay in the 'University of Freedom'.

The more I wrote the more I remembered and it got me thinking that every ex-prisoner should record their memoirs, either written or orally - God knows some would have a lot more to say than I do.

I met many characters and experienced many situations between 1984 and 1991 and I hope the following pages capture these.

It is by no means a definitive account or history of the Crum and The H-Blocks during my time there but rather an attempt to record my memories of the sometimes good times there, sometimes bad, sometimes sad but at all times, comradely.

Tá súil again go mbainfidh tú suit as

Faoi Ghlas

'The Crum'

On the 27th of July 1984, I was arrested along with Rab Henry and Basil Henry.

We were in possession of an undercar boobytrap bomb and a Smith and Wesson .38 revolver when the RUC swooped on us on the Ormeau Road at 2.30 a.m. After seven days of interrogation in Castlereagh, we appeared in Belfast Crown Court on Friday 3rd of August charged with possession of the weapon and explosives. We were immediately taken to Crumlin Road Jail. The three of us in one van, enclosed inside in our own individual tiny windowless compartment accompanied by the customary RUC escort.

As I peered out the small slit that served as a window, I stole only a fleeting glance at daily life in Belfast City centre. As people continued on their business of shopping, socialising and conversing, I thought of how my brothers and many others had gone the same journey in much the same manner as I was now doing.

We alighted from the van and two steps later we were in the prison reception area. A dimly lit, airless building that matched the welcome we received.

After being ordered to undress and wash in a bath full of eye watering disinfectant, we were photographed and fingerprinted. Any clothes we possessed of a dark colour were taken from us as was jewellery. I was given a prison identification number, 2212. This was my first encounter with a prison administration's attempts to dehumanise me.

We were ordered to follow several screws who led us through D' Wing and in behind huge doors. This area was known as the Base and

Faoi Ghlas

although I was glad to be out of Castlereagh, I was totally unprepared for the Base.

This part of the jail was used to hold prisoners until such times as the jail administration decided on which wing of the jail they would be held pending trial. Apart from the Base being dirty, colourless and lacking any fresh air the screws that staffed it were totally hostile - especially to Republicans.

They never spoke but yelled every last word. All this of course was designed to intimidate and frighten any newcomer to the place.

Upon arrival we were lined up outside the Governors' office for interview and told by the screw in charge that we were to address the Governor as Sir.

As we stood waiting to go in and see the Governor, another prisoner, not connected to us was returning to his cell. His hands were deep into his pockets when a screw thundered out,

"Get them fuckin' hands out of your fuckin' pockets."

I felt sorry for the man but made a mental note not to put myself in the same position!

The 'interview' with the Governor was short and sweet!

"2212 Adams, you will follow prison orders and rules and will not mix with 'paramilitary' prisoners. Tomorrow you will be transferred to A' Wing."

And then in a more pleasant tone to the screws;

"Take him away".

Faoi Ghlas

Shortly after this I was brought to my cell. A dank, dirty and unwelcoming room awaited me. Seconds later, one of my co-accused, Rab, arrived in behind me and I could see by the look on his face he wasn't too impressed either. Basil, whom I had never met prior to our arrest, was held several cells away.

Eighteen months earlier a Falls Road man had told me I would end up dead or in jail - how prophetic I thought as Rab and I sat down on our beds.

We hadn't seen each other since our arrest and soon we were swapping stories of interrogation techniques in Castlereagh and tales of woe around our arrest.

Our conversation was interrupted by a screw opening our cell door. He informed both Rab and I that we had a visit. Another screw then led us out of the Base, back through the administration circle and into the visiting area.

This was an open plan area with about a dozen tables. Each had three hard chairs. Space between visiting tables barely existed and this afforded visitor and prisoner little or no privacy. Two screws stood at opposite ends of the room and observed the goings-on. Occasionally they would patrol up and down the length of the room. Visits were tense enough occasions without screws hovering over you, watching every move and listening to every word.

Admittedly the situation changed through time, especially in the H-Blocks but in the Crum where the screws believed they had the upper hand on us, visiting conditions were extremely poor.

My Ma and our Paddy arrived into the visiting room. My Ma had a brave face on her but I knew that beneath the smile, her heart was breaking.

Faoi Ghlas

I was sorry for the heartache I was bringing to her. She was almost sixty years old but in a strong and determined voice she told me that my family were as one behind me and not to worry about anything. I knew this but it was still great to hear.

My Mother had been a republican all her life and had never once attempted to dissuade her children from being the same. With great dignity she visited each of her imprisoned sons as well as numerous other relations and friends who were held captive.

There are many Irish Mothers like her but I am very proud Annie Adams was mine.

My family have had a long affinity with jails and all of their trappings. Between us all we would have many stories to tell. One of my Mother's favourites centred on her preparing a food parcel to be left in on a visit to one of my brothers.

It was in the early seventies and I was about eight (I swear!).

We were in the kitchen of our house on the Whiterock Road and as she readied the parcel and I watched her put the chocolate biscuits into the brown bag, I asked her could I have that sort when I went to jail? Talk about tempting fate!

On the visit, our Paddy who had only been released six months earlier, made me aware of jail routines and procedures and of what to expect in the immediate days ahead of me.

He encouraged me to read and to think of how to escape.

Faoi Ghlas

ESCAPE!

I was only in the gate ("my coat was still swinging" as Skeet would say) and here was Paddy telling me how to get out. He then told me that when he had been there in '81, the boy's had hidden hacksaw blades above the pipes in the toilet in A 'wing and I should check if they were still there. I never ever told him, but I checked and they weren't.

Before very long the 30 minute visit was over. The screw placed the visiting pass on the table to signal this. I hugged both Paddy and my Mother before exiting one door and they another.

Back in the cell I read the newspapers that had been left into me in my parcel. I can't remember if I got the biscuits I requested all those years previous but I did get a book, The Singing Flame by Ernie O'Malley from our Gerry. I lent this to Robbie Laverty some months later but never ever saw it again - more to do with me being moved from one wing to another than Robbie keeping it but that was the way of books in jail. We were always seeking out new reading material and always lending and borrowing. Inevitably books went astray.

Before long it was dark and the night screw turned the light off by the switch outside our cell at what seemed an early hour.

Rab and I settled down to sleep but before doing so we scraped our names on the wall, low down in the corner, and well out of the screws' sight.

As I lay there, the circumstances of my arrest ran round my head like a long distance runner on an athletics track. Round and round and round.

I recalled Basil walking down the Ormeau Road to the site of our target with Rab not far behind him. I was about fifty yards behind Rab and just

Faoi Ghlas

approaching the Good Shepherd Convent when I noticed two cars pull out from a side street and immediately stop beside the two boys. There was a lot of shouting and as it was a fairly bright night I could clearly see the RUC men jump from the cars and approach Rab and Basil. Never mind 'caught by the henry's', here I was 'caught with the Henry's.'

My first instinct was to turn back up the Ormeau Road and as I did so I thought of climbing over the high wall surrounding the Convent but this thought soon vanished for as soon as I turned I was greeted by the unwelcome sight of another two RUC cars speeding down either side of the road towards me.

I could hear another speed up behind me and soon I was also surrounded. As they jumped from their cars the two closest to me shouted at me to stop. I turned to face them. One had a Ruger rifle pointed at me and the other a handgun. I raised my hands.

Down the back of my trouser waistband was my own handgun.

As they approached I was told to turn round and face the wall. This I did and one of them frisked me. On discovering the gun he shouted to his colleagues that I was armed and he pushed me to the ground. While doing this he retrieved the gun and two or three of them began to kick me as I lay there. Thankfully this didn't last very long and after asking for my name and address I was handcuffed and left lying down on the ground.

One Peeler had his foot on the side of my head pressing my face into the cold tarmac. I could smell the polish of his boots. For a second he removed his foot and I stole a glance down towards Rab and Basil. I could see one of them at the side of the cars but before I could work out who it was the Peeler with the polished boots hit me an unmerciful kick

Faoi Ghlas

in the face. Soon after this I was hauled into one of their cars and taken to Castlereagh.

I must have fallen off to sleep but it did not seem too long before I was awake again.

The sound of the key in the lock and the hard metal clang of the bolt being shot back by a screw greeted us as we were rustled from our sleep. With a grunt rather than a request we were quickly introduced to 'slopping out' - the out-dated practice of cleaning out your chamber pot into a large toilet bowl. The stench of the toilet area and the sensation of the smell of bleach and urine invading my nostrils is still clear in my mind.

We were then instructed by a screw to brush out our cell.

As we did so, I wondered did this constitute prison work. I thought of the Hunger Strikers and their refusal to do prison work.

I was totally unsure as to whether or not we should be doing this but we would soon be on the wing with republicans and in a friendlier environment such quandaries would be much easier to resolve.

Late in the morning of the 4th August I was escorted into A' Wing. This was the biggest wing in the Crum and like the other wings had three levels or landings as they were known in jail parlance.

In the middle of each wing stood a flight of stairs. These stairs ascended to the third landing. Prisoners were held on each side of the landing with republicans and loyalists in alternate cells. This was designed to prevent each group being immediately beside each other. The landings were joined by a huge metal wire net. This was suspended from the landings and was known as a suicide net.

Faoi Ghlas

The doors linking the circle with A' Wing closed behind me and as I entered the wing the noise level immediately struck me.

"A' Wing, one on"' thundered out the screw who was escorting me.

This indicated to the wing screws that they had a new arrival.

As I scanned the area seeking out a familiar face, another one of the screws indicated to me with a nod of his head and a gruff voice that I should follow him.

"This way Adams" he barked in my direction.

I followed and he walked me in the direction of the stairs.

Then without any warning he too yelled at the top of his voice, "A2, one on."

"Does nobody talk in here?" I asked myself

I was shown to cell 47 and as the screw placed the card bearing my name into the slot adjacent the cell door I noticed another card already there bearing the name of my soon to be cell mate.

I did not recognise the name but attempts to place a face to it were interrupted by the screw informing me that my "mates" were in the exercise yard if I wanted to go out to them. I assumed, correctly that my "mates" were fellow republicans and so I made my way out.

It was a bright, clear day as I exited the wing into the fresh air. It was my first breath of clean air in over a week and I was glad of it. I sheltered my eyes from the glare of the sun as I climbed the small steps that brought me up into the yard itself and into the welcoming company of republican prisoners.

Faoi Ghlas

The yard seemed huge. Occupied by about 150 prisoners, the grey walls surrounding it were topped with barbed wire and the prisoners walked in a continuous circuit of the four walls. Some set on the few benches available while others played soccer.

First to greet me was Eugene Gilmartin - the last time I saw him was two days before his arrest. He thrust his hand into mine in a firm grasp and as I spoke to Eugene, other familiar faces came into view. Among them Chopper and Hucker and I soon found myself relaxing in their company.

Two days before Chopper and Eugene were arrested, I had been in their company. They tried to persuade me to go for a drink with them later in the week in St Matthew's Social Club in the Short Strand. I declined the offer - drinking with 'Red Lights' (the term given to very well known republicans) was not encouraged. It was when returning from the Short Strand that they became involved in a confrontation with the UDR and were subsequently arrested and taken to Castlereagh. It was from there that they ended up in the Crum charged with killing a prison Governor.

Eugene explained to me that I would have to be debriefed about the circumstances of my arrest and subsequent interrogation. Details of this would be relayed to the Army on the outside. Eugene then introduced me to Gerry McAleenan, the man I would spend the next nine months with as my cell mate.

I never tired of Gerry's craic, he was always mixing and up to no good but was also a very serious person when it came to republicanism and prison issues.

That night the details of my debriefing were written on to cigarette papers and folded as small as possible before being wrapped in stretch and seal cling film and the ends sealed with a cigarette lighter to keep them waterproof. It was my first experience of a "comm"

Faoi Ghlas

(communication) or in gaeilge "teac" (teachaireacht) but from then, I don't think a day passed in the next seven years without me being in possession of one or more of these.

My experiences, mind you were not all good, as you will read later.

On my visit the day before, our Paddy had told me that it was likely I would get a cell raid from the screws the day after I arrived on the wing. Their intelligence system was aware of the debriefing sessions and they would hope to catch raw prisoners out.

I was a bit concerned about this and outlined my concerns to Gerry. He told me not to worry as he nodded off to sleep.

Worry I did! I mean it was bad enough being caught with a bomb and revolver without providing written confirmation of it.

True to form, bright and early the next morning the screws arrived in. Two of them dressed in overalls took Gerry out of the cell while another two searched me and whatever constituted as my property.

They were friendly and talkative at all times and I felt awkward being alone with them, as I did not know if I should engage them in conversation or not. (As months turned into years I learned when to talk to screws and when not to talk to them but that first encounter did leave me ill at ease).

Roles were then reversed and I was taken outside while Gerry was searched. The comm remained undetected.

Gradually over the next two or three months I slowly settled into my new surroundings. The 'good day - bad day' procedure was hard to comprehend at first. A new prisoner's first few days could be confusing

Faoi Ghlas

and it was not uncommon for them to get confused as to when they should be in the yard or canteen and when they should not be.

Mistakes could find one in the company of those whose company, one would wish to avoid!

The good day - bad day routine involved loyalist and republicans having the greater use of the canteen and yard areas on alternate days. This arrangement was agreed upon by the prisoners themselves in order to lessen any contact between republican and loyalist prisoners and amounted to a de facto segregation. The prison administration continually tried to integrate the two sets of prisoners and this was always resisted by republicans.

Any contact between ourselves and loyalists were carried out by the republican leadership (more commonly known as the jail staff) and on some occasions meetings between both republican and loyalist staffs would take place while one set of us were exercising in the yard. The prison administration were aware of these meetings but were powerless to stop them.

Any other contact was at the discretion of the O.C.

Five months before my arrest, our Gerry had been shot and seriously wounded by loyalists and two of the would be assassins, John Gregg and Gerard Walsh were also held in A' Wing. My cell was only yards away from theirs and I was cautioned by the O.C. that I should not allow myself to be duped into a confrontation with them. Some republicans wanted to attack Gregg and Walsh but were dissuaded from this by Gerry McCartney who was the O.C. at that time.

John Gregg was a huge man with a muscular body covered in tattoos. On his back was a tattoo of a fox chasing a rabbit. The rabbit was running

Faoi Ghlas

down Gregg's back in the direction of Gregg's anus! It was clear from his physique that he worked out in his cell but he never attempted to engage with me in any way.

Walsh on the other hand would nod to me if we crossed each others paths going to and from visits.

I ignored him but on one occasion we both had a visit at the same time. We were only yards apart and I was uncomfortable with this. Two of my sisters were up to see me and I was concerned for their safety once they left the prison.

I was sure Walsh would alert his visitors as to whom my visitors were and this would place them in danger. I waited to the end of my visit and told my sisters who Walsh was and to be careful on the way home. Thankfully nothing came of it.

The Crum was full of people from all over the six counties and from the south of Ireland as well. I met people whom I would never have met had it not been for our involvement in armed struggle and subsequent imprisonment. There were some people who took things in their stride and nothing seemed to bother them. There were also some very serious people who found imprisonment and the uncertainty of their future difficult to comprehend but all of us had one thing in common - if convicted we faced long periods of imprisonment in the H-Blocks.

To some of us, like those married with children, imprisonment meant a lot more than it did to young single men and of course, some of us hid the hardship better than others but when the cell door was closed behind us at night we all did our wack!

Every one of us looked forward to the regular visits from our family and friends. I had no shortage of these with my mother and five sisters, Margaret, Anne, Frances, Maura and Deirdre only too willing to fill the

Faoi Ghlas

three half hour visits we received each week. There was nothing my sisters wouldn't do for me while I was imprisoned.

Having a girl up on a visit was a big occasion too and was often the topic of conversation between prisoners for days on end. This would often lead to visits with other prisoner's sisters or someone supposed to be their sister!

It was not unknown for someone from one part of the country to produce a photo of a beautiful girl and to declare that his 'sister' wanted a visit with someone from another county. Immediately there would be a queue of people willing to write to this beautiful girl and subsequently send out a visit to her.

When the day of the visit arrived the comrade's nerves would be shattered but not shattered enough for them to spend thirty minutes in the shower and to shave themselves almost to the bone. The best of clothes would be donned and to cheers and backslaps from his 'friends' he would head off to the visit with this beautiful girl.

Imagine the shock when the beauty of the girl on the visit was the complete opposite of the one in the photo!

One Saturday morning in October, just as I thought I had come to know almost everyone in A' Wing, a screw opened our cell door and casually informed Gerry and I that we were being moved to C' Wing. At first the idea did not appeal to me at all but I could hardly tell that to the screws. Somehow I didn't think it would cut any ice.

Anyway a move it was but when we arrived in C Wing, much to our satisfaction, we once again ended up in the same cell! C' Wing was all but a smaller version of A' Wing but I found the craic much better. I believe this had a lot to do with all the republicans in C' Wing being in

Faoi Ghlas

the one canteen area at mealtimes, whereas in A' Wing we were separated into three canteens on each separate landing. The downside of the C' Wing canteen was the noise level.

At times it would have driven you to the sanctuary of your cell! Between people playing pool, table tennis and darts and with the television volume at its height the crescendo was deafening. Against all this some comrades were attempting to learn gaeilge in the corner - how they concentrated was beyond me.

My mate Tuso was there in C Wing as was Micky Mul and Spud. Big Gerry was in his element and soon he was up to his neck in playing mixes on people. There was no-one untouchable as far as he was concerned, although one senior staff member, Spud, took exception to being likened to the famous diarist, Samuel Pepys.

Extracts from a diary, allegedly owned by Spud were used as evidence by the Crown Prosecution to hold him on remand for two years and when Gerry had a request played for him on Radio Ulster's John Bennet show under the pseudonym of Samuel Pepys it did not go down too well.

Spud was livid with anger the following morning but of course this only served to have him nicknamed 'Pepys'. Fortunately for Spud the 'evidence' did not stand up in court and he was released at his trial.

As I said earlier, Gerry was always mixing and one mix in particular went on for weeks and almost ended up being reported to the Army on the outside.

The victim, Kevin Casey from Cookstown was a very likeable easygoing man who spoke with a deep country accent.

Paddy McCotter from Lenadoon had just been released after a short remand and Joe Haughey had taken over from Paddy as O.C. of the jail.

Faoi Ghlas

Word was sent over to this effect from A'Wing to C'Wing. Gerry received the comm and re-wrote it to read that Casey was to be O.C. Casey was thrilled to hear this piece of scéal but couldn't work out how the IRA should choose him. Gerry re-assured him that it was on account of his track record prior to his arrest and the Army 'was obviously impressed with this'.

Gerry told Casey that he must keep this information strictly confidential and that all would be revealed in due course.

On hearing of his 'promotion', Casey pulled back his broad shoulders, puffed out his chest and willingly accepted his appointment as Officer Commanding. From that moment on he seemed to almost float round the yard and it was quite obvious that he had swallowed the bait, hook, line and sinker.

I can still recall his bright red face glowing brighter each step of their journey as Gerry led him on a merry dance round the yard and filled him full of shite as regards his responsibilities as O.C.

Part of this responsibility entailed Casey to keep in regular contact with the Army. And through whom was the channel to the Army? Why Gerry of course!!!

After a week of 'communication', Gerry informed Casey that the Army planned an escape and Casey was to lead it!

Now Casey knew in his heart that the 'evidence' against him (he had been charged with possession of a two thousand pound landmine) was not all that convincing and that the chances of him walking out at his trial were fair to middling.

He enclosed this information in his next comm to the Army and asked them to contact his solicitor if they needed legal advice on the matter.

Faoi Ghlas

Gerry read the comm out to me that night in our cell and I honestly didn't know whether to laugh or cry!

Gerry, in a very sternly worded reply told Casey that it was the sworn duty of every P.O.W. to escape and Casey, as a 'leader of men' must lead by example.

However, Casey was not impressed!

He had a girlfriend, Kathleen, and he didn't believe escaping would enhance his relationship with her.

Besides that, he could possibly beat the charges, so why escape? His mind was made up and he wrote back to the Army.

It went something like:

"Comrades, I received your comm but with some reluctance I must inform you that I will not be able to lead the escape as I have my feet firmly under the table with Kathleen and I don't think she would be best pleased."

Now when Gerry read this out to me that night I was doubled over with laughter. There were tears in his eyes as he struggled against the laughing to complete the reading.

The sight of this was hilarious but amid the laughter, I felt a certain amount of trepidation. I had visions of Casey punching Gerry.

Casey was well and truly sucked in and I wondered what he would do when he found out the right way of things. Would he see the funny side or would he indeed punch Gerry?

What would you do?

Faoi Ghlas

Soon after this, the matter was taken out of our hands when Casey confided his anxiety to one of his comrades from Tyrone. The comrade realised it was a mix and being none too impressed decided to write out to his local IRA ceannfort (O.C.) regarding the matter and he also informed Spud of the situation.

Spud got the hold of Gerry and told him in no uncertain terms to end the mix there and then. I caught Spud's eye during this and thought it best to avoid him for a while.

Later in the day I watched as Gerry walked round the yard with Casey and he told him the right way of things. Occasionally, both of them would laugh and Casey's face would redden as he heard the sceal from Gerry.

Thankfully he saw the funny side of it and although he swore revenge, nothing ever materialised. The comrade did not write out and P. O'Neill (pseudonym for the IRA) never had to write in.

I met Casey in Carrickmore at the Easter Sunday Parade about 2003 and we had a laugh about it all. The 'evidence' against him didn't stand up in court; he was released and still has his feet under the table!!

The population of Crumlin Road Gaol had been hugely increased in the early to mid 1980s through the use of the 'Paid Perjurer' or it was more commonly known the Supergrass system. The RUC, having arrested and interrogated some Republicans, would entice these Republicans to appear in court as prosecution witnesses against former comrades. Among those being held were many members of the Irish National Liberation Army (INLA). This organization was renowned for the disunity amongst its members and for a period in the Crum there were many fights among members of the INLA.

I found this very disheartening.

Faoi Ghlas

The ridiculous behavior only came to an end after a huge free for all in A' Wing left several of them severely injured and which was followed by an ultimatum from the IRA O.C. that either the fighting stops or they leave the Republican wings.

My first Christmas in jail was fairly uneventful. It was our 'good day' so we had what was described as a 'fry' in the canteen that morning. Our dinner wasn't much to get excited about either and that night was the usual noise filled session in the canteen. Afterwards in our cell Gerry and I tucked into the many chocolates we had been sent in as part of our Christmas Parcel. We were allowed chocolate and sweets in our parcels at Christmas and Easter but no other time.

Christmas Eve had been slightly more eventful however. Gerry had been having a long running dispute with this particular screw who had taken a dislike to him. He thrived on confrontation with them - he told me it got his day in. Both our families (and friends) had sent many Christmas cards into us and we had them up all over the cell walls. This was achieved by tearing thread from the blankets and attaching this to the wall before hanging our cards over it. On the afternoon of Christmas Eve, just as the last post had been delivered and no more cards would be coming in and, as we were admiring our decor, the screw with whom Gerry had been having the dispute arrived at our cell door and told us we were moving cell!

This meant all the cards having to be taken down off the walls and they and all our belongings moved to our new cell. Needless to say we were not amused but not to be outdone we worked late into the night and managed to put every card back up, almost in the same manner as they had been in our previous cell.

Easter Sunday 1985 was a good day. As republicans we were not going to be deterred from remembering our patriot dead and plans were

Faoi Ghlas

made for a parade in the yard. The screws were aware of our plans as a similar parade took place every year. Gerry and I smuggled a Tricolour in that had been sewn into the lining of his coat. He wore the coat to the yard that day and once outside and past the screws we removed the flag as the rest of the lads fell in for the parade. We all wore our best shoes, perfectly shined and our coats were adorned with prison made Easter Lillies held securely in place with a pin.

Of course it was possible that the screws would send the riot squad into the yard and disrupt us but they normally adopted a policy of attempting to identify those carrying out roles and after lock-up, charge them with a breach of 'discipline'.

Fitzy, who was the O.C. of C Wing at the time, had asked me to re-enact the reading of the 1916 Easter Proclamation during the parade. This had first been read by Pádraig Pearse on the steps of the General Post Office in Dublin and heralded the start of the Rising. I considered this an honour. The night before I had copied the Proclamation onto cigarette papers for easy transfer inside my mouth to the yard. It was agreed that those carrying out roles would stay to the back of the gathering where we would be sheltered somewhat from the screw's vision.

When given the nod, I took a half step forward and in my best voice I re-enacted Padraig Pearse and proclaimed the Republic. My heart was beating fast but unfaltering I read each word and at the finish stepped back into line.

The screws never came across the flag and we smuggled it back out the following week in much the same manner as we smuggled it in.

In August 1985 I reached the end of my first year in the Crum. There was no sign of my trial. My remand period had ended and my prison status was now officially awaiting trial. I had no expectation of a trial before

Faoi Ghlas

1986 but I knew the longer I spent in the Crum the less I would spend in the Blocks though the uncertainty of it all, at times, did your head in.

Comrades were being sentenced almost on a weekly basis and this obviously had an effect on your morale. Everyday we got sceal that such and such a person had received a trial date and the judge at their trial was going to be a real bastard who handed out the heaviest sentences. In reality they were all real bastards and sentencing or the length of sentences were determined to a large extent by the political climate on the outside.

If the Army had just let off a thousand pound bomb the day before your trial or a number of British Crown Forces had been killed it was pretty certain your sentence would be increased by two or three years.

There were also huge discrepancies when it came to sentences for republican and loyalist prisoners with some republicans being sentenced to almost twice as long as loyalists for similar activities.

On a similar note I remember one loyalist, Joe McAuley from Sandy Row, being granted compassionate parole to spend Christmas with his daughter who was 'missing' him! That one really irked me.

Christmas 1985 came and went. I was now sharing a cell with Paul Smith from Fermanagh. Smitty, as he was called was great craic. He had literally just turned seventeen when arrested and charged with killing a British soldier.

When the killing took place, Smitty was only thirteen!

I remember his mother being a very friendly person and she developed a close bond with my own mother. Having a son in prison was a whole new experience for Marjorie and she took strength and comfort from my mother's experiences.

Faoi Ghlas

Often our visits would take place on the same day and both our mothers would meet in the waiting areas and swap stories. Smitty was totally innocent of the charge and one of many, many people framed and imprisoned by the corrupt system in Ireland.

On Smitty's second day in jail, the boys told him that an escape had been planned for that day. Some prisoners were to climb over the wall using rope ladders and a distraction was required. He was asked to fake an epileptic fit in front of the screws watchtower in order to provide this distraction.

Smitty agreed and when the signal was given, Smitty, in his best acting mode, dropped to the ground and began flailing his arms and legs round in every direction. After a minute or so he realised no escape was taking place and as he rose from the ground he was greeted with cheers from the rest of us. His face was beetroot red but he saw the funny side and within weeks, he was up to his neck in carrying out similar mixes and winding new prisoners up.

The nature of the remand system in Crumlin Road was such that a prisoner could spend up to two years awaiting trial and in some cases a lot of prisoners spent over three years.

It was agonising not knowing what sentence you would receive and the lengthy periods between arrest and eventual sentencing only increased the agony. It also ratcheted the pressure on the individual and led to many disputes between comrades.

The biggest source of dispute for many people was the issue of pleading guilty or not guilty to the charge of which they were accused.

Pleading guilty, in general, resulted in a lesser sentence but in doing so, one accepted the 'right' of a British court to operate in a part of Ireland.

Faoi Ghlas

This led to many arguments and many theories for and against a particular plea. It is probably true to say that most people brought pressure to bear upon themselves by taking a rigid stance on the issue.

The best advice I received was from our Paddy who told me that if I pleaded not guilty and never carried out another piece of republican activity again in my life that no-one could question me as I had followed every republican directive while imprisoned.

In my time in Crumlin Road I took part in many arguments with people who subsequently pleaded guilty. In some arguments I questioned their republican credentials and if truth were told I was not very comradely. Things were said that should not have been said and I take this opportunity now to withdraw those comments and apologise for any hurt I may have caused.

The coming and going of prisoners was relentless and we came across all sorts. Some of these were people imprisoned as a result of issues, which had nothing whatsoever to do with the conflict.

The procedure with those accused of non-conflict related actions coming onto republican wings operated along these lines. If the accused person's charge was not of a serious or violent nature and he was not a threat to republicans, and was almost certain to receive bail after two or three days, it was not uncommon for the person to be allowed to stay on the wing until bail was granted.

If the opposite was the case the person was asked to leave the wing. The screws knew this to be the case and sometimes they would attempt to set up hoods or sex offenders and send them out into the exercise yard while republicans occupied it.

The plan was that the republicans would assault the prisoner and satisfy the screw's lust for the wrong doer to be injured.

Faoi Ghlas

In the time I was there I cannot recall republicans succumbing to this. Non-republicans were questioned by the I.O. as to their charges and then told to leave the wings if they were thought unsuitable.

Once this happened they would be brought to a non-political wing (in this case B'Wing) by the screws where they served out their time in a punitive and brutal environment.

Loyalist prisoners would allow some non-political prisoners to remain on their wing in order to boost their numbers. Others however, such as sex offenders, ran the risk of being beaten and dehumanised. Often the screws would be deliberately slow in their attempts to venture out to the yard and 'rescue' them.

In the Crum of course you met lots of people you would not have met if political circumstances had not dictated otherwise.

Some were very sound and some were plain crackpots.

I wasn't in very long when this fella (I will call him Jim -I cannot remember his actual name) arrived in. We were out in the yard at the time and as he walked round the yard, the I.O. fell in beside him and began to search out the charges that Jim faced.

Jim communicated to the I.O. that he was deaf and dumb.

Colm McLaughlin from Buncrana indicated to the I.O. that he knew sign language and was soon employed to find out Jim's circumstances. After a period of various hand movements (having absolutely no clue of what was being communicated did not deter the rest of us watching with great interest) Colm reported back to the I.O. that Jim was indeed deaf and dumb, that his charges were minor and he was sure to get bail the following day. On the strength of this it was decided Jim could stay on the wing until his bail appearance.

Faoi Ghlas

An hour or so later Jim was sitting on the bench along the back wall of A' Wing when an announcement bellowed out from the tannoy speaker system.

"Visit for Jim Smith. Jim Smith report to landing for visit."

Immediately Jim rose from the bench and walked towards the landing before quickly realizing his slip-up and running the last 15 yards.

He was never seen (or heard of) again. We never quite worked out his rationale and he certainly didn't strike us as your average British intelligence agent but the episode led to much banter between Colm and the I.O.

On another occasion a man arrived on to our wing late on the Saturday afternoon. He said he had been arrested by the Brits in South Armagh. He went onto tell some of us that he was a very active republican who had served time in Portlaoise Prison.

I found it strange that he did not know the likes of Lucas Quigley or Fat Campbell (two Ballymurphy men in Portlaoise at that time) but as it was Saturday and we would have no opportunity for contact with the Army outside until Tuesday (no visits took place on a Monday) we decided to wait until then and check things out.

Tuesday came and our friend went for bail: before doing so he borrowed jeans, a jumper and a coat from various people. Later in the afternoon it emerged that he was actually a conman who had walked into a Belfast car showroom and drove out in a brand new sports car after asking for a test drive.

The judge ordered he be driven to the Armagh - Louth border by the RUC and barred from entering the North - needless to say he did not return the borrowed clothes.

Faoi Ghlas

Frankie Curry was a loyalist prisoner from Bangor. He had plenty of jail experience and made much of telling me that he had been in the Crum

in 1981 with our Paddy and together with Bobby Storey they had 'run the place'. He would also frequently slide The Belfast Telegraph under my cell door for me to read.

Curry was responsible for a small explosion in the yard of C Wing in 1985. A screw picked up a cigarette packet that loyalists had left behind them and it exploded slightly injuring the screw. That night I heard a voice whispering through the gap at the side of my cell door.

It was Curry boasting how they had sorted out the screws and would take no shit. I reminded him that Loyalists probably knew where a lot of screws lived and they could 'sort them out' a lot more effectively if they really wished.

Shortly after this there was a report of another bomb in the toilet of C Wing. The screws were understandably cagey and called for the British army bomb squad to deal with this. I was in a cell on my own at this time not far from the toilet when I heard the commotion outside on the landing.

I got off the bed, moved to the door and pressed my head as close to the gap between the cell door frame and the wall as I could. This afforded me a glimpse of two British soldiers walking in the direction of the toilet.

They passed out of view and though I could hear them speak, above the noise of loyalists yelling at them and republicans trying to relay to each other what was happening, I could not clearly make out what they were saying.

My head was pushed tight to the metal door; almost glued on to it when suddenly there was a small explosion from the toilet. The Brits had

Faoi Ghlas

blown up the 'suspicious package' and the blast had reverberated down the wing knocking my head off the door and against the wall. I didn't know whether to laugh or cry. There were a lot of Derry people in the

Crum at this time being held on the word of a 'Paid Perjurer'. Eddie McSheffrey was one of them.

Eddie was a very small, bespectacled man with a huge personality. It was close to Christmas 1984 when the evidence being given against Eddie by Raymond Gilmour was rejected by the court and Eddie accompanied by his co-accused were released.

In early 1986 I was walking round C Wing yard when Eddie arrived in again. It was absolutely freezing and he had no coat. He walked with the aid of crutches after having being seriously injured in an explosion in which another IRA Volunteer, Charles English died.

It was good to see Eddie again and he quickly fell in behind the Army structures and soon found himself on the jail staff. He told me he would beat this charge too as evidence against him was scarce. True to form he did.

In October 1987 I heard on the radio that two Derry IRA Volunteers had been killed in a premature explosion. Eddie McSheffrey was one of them. Several days later, baton-wielding RUC members, in an attempt to prevent the IRA firing a volley of shots over the coffins of Eddie and his comrade Paddy Deery attacked their funerals. The Volunteers succeeded in this final salute, much, I am sure, to Eddie's delight.

Another man I became very friendly with was Terry 'Cleaky' Clarke. I had heard of Cleaky but had never met him. In 1985 he arrived into the Crum on trumped up kidnapping charges. Cleaky had tonnes of prison experience behind him and soon began to use it to improve our lot.

Faoi Ghlas

Dominic with his brothers Gerry, Paddy and Seán in the tunnel between Crumlin Road Jail and the Courthouse 2008

Faoi Ghlas

Our inexperience was illustrated clearly when it came to our handling of internal prison courts. If a republican prisoner was charged with a breach of prison rules, that republican would appear in front of a prison Governor who would act as a judge.

Screws would give their 'evidence' and the republican would refuse to make any plea or take part in the proceedings, therefore leaving the Governor no option but to find him guilty and sentence him to the punishment wing or more commonly known as the boards.

One such incident occurred in the summer of 1985. The screws had removed some prisoner's radios from their cells while they had been in the canteen. These radios had been previously brought out to the exercise yard - this was considered a 'breach of prison rules'.

In a conversation with a comrade while waiting at the canteen gate I was overheard by a screw making a comment that amounted to us needing to do something about it.

This was interpreted as incitement and as I refused to partake in the 'court proceedings' I spent three days on the boards. Cleaky thought we were foolish and advised us to plead not guilty when in front of the prison court.

He encouraged us to request legal advice and legal representation at the courts. Soon our solicitors were appearing for us and the screws' evidence was being contradicted.

Eyewitnesses were being called and screws had to think twice before charging someone. Cleaky had a long running battle with the screws and never once allowed them to get on top of him. He successfully challenged the prison administration's refusal to allow him the right to wear a tie on his visits and struck a fine appearance as he walked out to his visit with Mary Doyle.

Faoi Ghlas

He also had a notion that the screws were stealing biscuits from his weekly parcel. On his visit Cleaky would know exactly how many biscuits Mary had left in and when collecting the parcel he would take every biscuit out and count them in front of the screw.

This really got up the screws nose, especially as Cleaky would refuse to sign for the parcel and would demand to see the screw's superior. Soon the correct number of biscuits was being delivered but this, in turn, only led to Cleaky looking for something else with which to torture the screws.

Cleaky was released in 1985 after the charges were withdrawn but he soon found himself back in jail again in 1988. While in the H-Blocks, he was diagnosed with cancer but having served his sentence, he once again, upon his release, returned to the republican struggle. There he worked until his untimely death.

Fuair Cleaky bas I Mi Meitheamh 2000. B'fhear maith e.

Faoi Ghlas

The Trial

In February 1986, I received notification from my solicitor, P.J. McGrory that my trial was set for Tuesday 3rd of March. I had been granted a separate trial from my co-accused, Rab and Basil who had both been sentenced to twelve years imprisonment on the 14th of February. It was during this time that Unionists were protesting against the signing of the Anglo-Irish Agreement (an agreement between the London and Dublin governments designed to undermine support for Sinn Fein by promoting constitutional nationalism).

I was naturally concerned for the safety of my family who would be attending my trial.

I was also very concerned as to how long a sentence I would receive. There was never any likelihood I would be found not guilty and be released and P.J. telling me I could get twenty years was not very comforting.

The day arrived and I was brought through the underground tunnel linking Crumlin Road Prison and Crumlin Road Courthouse. When I arrived in the dock I could see my mother and sisters in the public gallery and they smiled and waved at me.

The presiding judge was Andrew Donaldson (a former member of the RUC) and a person not renowned for leniency towards republicans. Donaldson had sentenced Dessie Collins from Andersonstown to twenty-two years not long before my trial.

The prosecution presented their case that I was involved in a conspiracy to kill a member of the RUC and that I was arrested in possession of a .38 Smith and Wesson revolver and an under car booby trap bomb. Two years previously a similar type of bomb had been found under a car owned by Donaldson himself.

Faoi Ghlas

The arresting RUC officers preceded to describe my arrest (neglecting to mention the beating of course) and the detectives who interrogated me while in Castlereagh followed them.

The forensic 'experts' described what effect the bomb would have had if it had exploded and when they turned to the issue of the .38 revolver, I remember Donaldson taking it from them and examining it as he sat in his chair.

He seemed to revel in this examination, almost as if he was enjoying the feel of the weapon and gloating at its capture.

Soon it was the turn of the defence and I don't think Donaldson was too impressed when my counsel offered 'no defence' to the prosecution case.

All that the prosecution had said was true but I didn't feel it my place to be confirming any of it or saving the courts' time by admitting to it.

I was found guilty after a trial lasting one and three quarter hours and put back for sentencing until the following Friday.

The time until then crawled in. I had two visits with my mother on the two days running up to the sentencing and she did her best to settle my nerves.

When the Friday arrived, I bade farewell to my comrades in the Crum and once again was brought over through the tunnel and into the cells below the court house.

P.J. spoke to me very quickly there and shook my hand before I was led into the dock. From there I could see my mother and my sisters sitting several rows away. Donaldson entered from his chambers and

Faoi Ghlas

proceedings began. By now my nerves had settled and I awaited the outcome.

I was glad I was about to put the previous nineteen months in the Crum behind me and I was actually looking forward to the Blocks and seeing a lot of old friends.

After some legal points and final submissions, Donaldson began his summing up by telling me that I should not expect any credit for having wasted the courts' time.

I didn't expect any.

After shuffling through legal papers on his bench, Donaldson looked at me and loudly proclaimed;

"Fourteen years on all charges."

I was relieved it wasn't higher and then I felt P.J. shake my hand as the screws rushed me out of the court.

I caught a glimpse of my mother and waved at her.

As I was leaving the court I heard our Anne shout out to me,

"Dominic, tiocfaidh ar la".

At the top of my voice I shouted back, "Up the 'RA" and before I knew it I was back in the cells underneath the courthouse.

On my way to the cells I passed one of the RUC detectives from Castlereagh and the disappointment that I didn't receive more of a sentence was written all over his face!

Faoi Ghlas

That afternoon, I was brought back to the Base to await my transfer to the H-Blocks. This time, things were different. The screws and their attitudes were the same but nineteen months of prison soon teaches you new tricks.

I believe the screws knew this also and so they reserved their bullying tactics for new prisoners and I was left alone.

Faoi Ghlas

The H-Blocks

Next morning, Saturday 8th March 1986, I was transported in a windowless van to the H-Blocks. Through a small chink of light in the back I could make out the M1 motorway and the surrounding fields. The journey didn't last very long and the thought of going to the Blocks did not fill me with any big sense of dread.

We soon arrived and I listened at the door, as one set of screws exchanged my details with another set of screws and then the doors were opened and I was ushered out of the van.

The first thing I noticed while walking to the H-Blocks reception was the sense of space and light. Everything in the Crum had been conducted in a small tight confined space with no sight of the outside. Here as I walked the small distance from the van to the reception area I caught a good long glimpse of the spring sky and felt the chill of the cold air. I felt good.

The processing itself was very quick. Fingerprints taken, photo taken and wing allocation lasted no time at all. I was allocated a wing and told my transport would be along soon.

At this time in 1986 the prison administration was still attempting to integrate republican prisoners with loyalist and conforming prisoners in what were known as mixed wings. Newly sentenced republican prisoners were well briefed before being sentenced on what to expect upon arrival in these wings and we were very clear on the appropriate steps to take in order to overcome this attempted integration.

When the circumstances dictated, republican prisoners also approached screws who worked on mixed wings (but occasionally found themselves

Faoi Ghlas

on a republican wing) and warned them against making it difficult for newly sentenced republicans to get off the mixed wings.

Our instructions were that upon arrival in the mixed wing we were to make it clear to the screw in charge that we did not intend to stay there and that we would assault the first prisoner we encountered. I was well psyched up for this and the implications.

When I entered the wing I began to tell the screw who was recording my arrival in the wing diary that I had no intentions of staying on the wing when he interrupted me.

"Look", he said "I don't care if you stay or not but if you don't want to stay I will have to charge you with threatening behaviour and you will end up on the boards and the punishment wing."

"Fair enough" I said, and that was that. I didn't have to raise my voice never mind my hand. To my amazement the screw then tried to persuade me against going to the boards on that day as it was a Saturday and I would only end up spending an extra day there waiting for the Governor to come in to work the following Monday and deal with my 'threatening behaviour'.

I declined his offer and soon I was on my way to the boards. The first step on the road to a republican wing had been completed.

I slept soundly that night and woke bright and early on the Sunday to one of the most memorable moments of my time in prison.

Around mid morning a screw opened the cell door and asked me did I wish to go to mass. Time out of the cell I thought to myself and away I went. I was brought out and told to get into the back of the van parked outside.

Faoi Ghlas

This I did and there sitting across from me was a man dressed in 1970s style clothing! My first reaction was to look away from him and at the floor, as I feared my expression would betray my thoughts but in doing so I immediately noticed he was wearing bright red football socks right up to his knees.

I could see they reached his knees as the jeans he wore only started at this point. He also wore a brown corduroy jacket with his two hands pushed deep into the pockets. His huge mop of hair bounced back and forth as he moved his head to speak to me.

I had the impression that my friend could not choose between the hairstyle of Noddy Holden or Leo Sayer and decided to incorporate both onto his head.

"Alright mo chara" he said, "You must be Dominic."

Surprised that he knew me, I answered that I was.

He told me his name was Basil Hardy from Ardoyne and that he had heard of my sentencing just before being put on the boards himself the previous Friday and had been expecting to meet me there. I found out he had been in prison from 1974 and it was very clear his 1974 fashion sense had not moved on from then.

Basil had been imprisoned in the 'Cages' part of Long Kesh where the prisoners were openly treated as political prisoners. Basil had decided, as had many other republicans round this time that their interests would be better served by transferring to the H-Blocks and thus had went through the same mixed wing procedure as myself.

We had a good yarn and he assured me that the boards and punishment wings were simply formalities and I would soon be on a republican wing.

Faoi Ghlas

Mass ended and I was soon back in my cell. I constantly thought of Basil and the length of time he had served. I had asked him when he expected to get out and he answered that he didn't have a clue.

It was hard to digest that here was someone in jail 12 years with no release in sight and I was only starting my sentence. Only those who experience it (and their close relatives) truly understand the reality of prison life. I thought I did until I met the many people who were already imprisoned, some for periods of up to fourteen years, when I first entered the H-Blocks.

I admire their families and how they stood by their sons and daughters for such incredible lengths of time and I have no fear in saying now, that as I thought about Basil that night, his time served frightened me (not to mention his clothes style) and brought home to me the harsh reality of prison life.

Next morning, 10th March, I was brought in front of a prison Governor called Smith. I remembered him from the Crum and he remembered me. I gave him the republican line of not mixing with loyalist prisoners and criminals etc and he simply nodded as I spoke.

I was sentenced to three days on the boards and four days isolation on the punishment wing. This passed uneventfully with the screws going out of their way to be courteous, if not friendly and on St Patrick's Day 1986, I was brought to D' Wing H-Block 5.

The H-Blocks were totally different in design from the Victorian prison design of the Crum. They had only one storey as opposed to three and the administrative 'circle' was actually a rectangle. This area formed the centre of the H-Block and the two sides were split into two wings each - A and B wing on one side and C and D wing on the other. Republicans were held in two of the wings on one side of the H and loyalists or non-

Faoi Ghlas

political prisoners on the other. There were eight of these in total and in affect they represented eight separate prisons situated inside one large prison camp.

The wing in each leg of the Block seemed very narrow and smaller in comparison to the wide wings in the Crum and as I carried my possessions down the wing I scanned the faces for anyone familiar.

I knew loads of republican prisoners but could not see any of them there. Just as panic was about to set in a slightly built man approached me and introduced himself as Leonard Ferrin and said he was the wing O.C. or, as gaeilge, the Ceannfort. He introduced me to others like Mickey-John, Ta Buck and Terry McLaughlin.

I was made very welcome by the rest of the boys and some of them helped me unpack my stuff. Others offered me the use of batteries for my radio or stamps for my letters.

A soccer match had been arranged for that afternoon in the yard and I was invited to play. This was the start of a love affair with soccer in the Blocks but more of that later! After the match I found it hard to take in how the boys, without seeking permission from a screw, simply went back to their already opened cells, picked up their towels and headed off en masse to the shower area.

After this we headed into the canteen where fellow republicans, as opposed to screws were putting out the dinner and afterwards other republicans, voluntarily and what seemed quite naturally washed up the dishes.

It was very clear that republican prisoners generally dictated their living circumstances and not the administration which was very much the case in the Crum.

Faoi Ghlas

That night Leonard, after he made us coffee and borrowed biscuits from the wing's quartermaster, invited me down to his cell and we spoke for a while on the set-up of the camp. Uppermost in his run-down, Leonard emphasised that the differences in conditions faced by republicans in the Blocks as opposed to the Crum were not willingly handed over by the prison administration.

Rather they were won by the sacrifices of the Hunger Strikers and the determination of republican POWs to resist any attempt by the prison administration to claw back the gains won then. Leonard was adamant that it wouldn't stop there - that republicans would continue to campaign and organise until they had secured conditions that allowed them to enjoy a quality of life suited to political prisoners and their needs.

Plans were made for further discussions dealing with the Blanket protest, Hunger Strike, the campaign for segregation from loyalists, the 1983 escape and future plans.

Over the next few months I settled into my new surroundings, made new friends and developed a regime that would hopefully see me through the remainder of my time there.

Life in the Blocks was totally different to what I had experienced in the Crum. The majority of time in the Crum was spent wondering how long a sentence you would get. The constant distraction of a pending trial was not conducive to settling ones' nerves and you barely thought beyond your trial date and pending sentence if convicted.

Concentration on other issues such as education was difficult.

In the Blocks you were aware of your sentence - you could plan your time - education courses were available from the administration and these were widely encouraged by republicans. There was also informal

Faoi Ghlas

education made available by the republican camp staff. These dealt with Irish history, republicanism and revolutionary conflicts throughout the world.

I threw myself headfirst into reading and read anything I could get my hands on. This led to me torturing my visitors for books. Our Gerry was a regular supplier of reading material. I only ever received one visit from him in seven years but plenty of books - though our Paddy claims it was really he who bought them - Gerry only signed them!

Soon I had developed a system where I read a book dealing with politics, Irish history or other colonial situations. Upon completion of this particular book I would then read a novel in order to wind down from the heavy concentration on the previous read.

James Connolly's writings were tremendous. The man was so far ahead of his time it was unbelievable. Others that spring to mind are The Tunnels of Cu Chi, Sandino's Daughters and a History of the Irish Working Class.

Stephen King novels were always a good bet for getting the head showered and escaping (if only in mind) from your surroundings. Strumpet City was a good read too.

I set about learning my native language with great enthusiasm. One of the biggest changes I noticed on arrival in the Blocks was not only the amount of Irish being spoken but the affect it had on the screws. They simply hadn't a clue what we were saying as the following example illustrates.

Two republican wings were situated along one leg of each H shaped block. At the end of these wings a huge gate would indicate the furthest point a prisoner could go. A space of about ten feet would separate the

Faoi Ghlas

two wings and in here a screw would sit and control movement between the two wing gates.

It was a very common sight for a republican to be standing at each gate and having a full-scale conversation as gaeilge. The screw had no idea whatsoever of what was being said.

Imagine having to listen to two people you have been told to fear at all costs and you don't know what they are saying? Sure they could be planning anything!!

I found this brilliant and decided there and then I would learn mo theanga féin.

Chomh maith le seo, bhiodh se tabhachtach le bheith ag caint as gaeilge nuair a bhiodh cuairt agat. Chuirti ar gcuid teachtaireactai tri na cuairteanna agus bhitea abalta a labhairt os comhair na caoimheadoiri agus na fir bui gan eolas a thabairt doibh.

Séamais Ó Hearáin from Hannahstown, a GAA enthusiast and Irish language muinteoir came in every week and taught us up to GCSE standard. His brother Brendan and my sister Deirdre married into the same family and he kept me up to date on all the scéal.

His son Raymond now teaches my son in Grammar school.

About a month after arriving into H5, we were locking up for the night and I had just settled down to read the Irish News and have a cup of tea. Suddenly I could hear Ta Buck shouting out through the gap between his cell door and the wall.

"Did you's get that sceal on the radio there?"

"No, lean ar aghaidh." came the replies.

Faoi Ghlas

I listened intently and what I heard sent shivers down my spine.

"There was a nuclear attack on Russia tonight and thousands are dead."

I thought he would soon shout out that he was joking but to no avail. For the next few minutes I waited quietly for the nine o'clock news. During this time, I had visions of Russian nuclear bombs being directed at America and Europe while American bombs rained down on the USSR.

I also had visions of the screws abandoning us to our fate. Somehow I did not expect them to be worried as to whether or not we survived a nuclear war. For a second, I thought if I closed the windows, I could keep the radiation out.

The news arrived and the newscaster reported that there had been a radiation leak at a nuclear plant in Chernobyl, near Russia. No mention of an attack!!!

Needless to say Ta Buck took some ribbing for this.

Incorrect reporting of scéal was a common occurrence in jail. One story I like concerns the report of a British soldier being shot dead in Kilnasaggart. It was passed down the wing and by the time it reached the bottom it had been transformed into a British soldier shooting dead a Sagart.

Sagart is the Irish word for priest and this Irish term was used more by us than the English word.

After a few months in H5 I was considered trustworthy enough to take a role in the intelligence-gathering department. This involved me familiarising myself with screw routines and engaging them in conversations on a daily basis. This was designed to lure them into a false sense of security and leave them vulnerable to slip-ups.

Faoi Ghlas

Shortly after this I was given a beart (Irish word for parcel) to mind overnight. This contained material which was useful to the I.O. department.

As I went to sleep that night I put it inside my pillowcase and slept with my hand inside the pillowcase also. Next morning, I awoke and headed off down to the shower - without the beart! I completely forgot about it!

As I have already said, republicans managed the everyday affairs of their wings and this particular day was the day for laundry change, i.e. the sheets and pillowcases were sent out to the circle area for laundry and changing.

Imagine my horror when I returned to the cell after my shower and not only was the sheets and pillowcase away but so too was the beart. It was like losing a dump outside!

The first person I saw as I rushed out to the wing was Tic Tac. I explained what happened and he set off at a gallop down to where the laundry would be stacked at the top of the wing but it was too late. It had already been moved to the circle.

Despite our best efforts we were unable to retrieve the laundry back onto the wing and as the day passed my mood darkened and darkened. Nothing could cheer me up.

I wrote to Ginty, the camp I.O. and told him I wanted to resign my position but he wrote back telling me to wise up.

That afternoon I had a visit and Bob Mór was in the next visiting cubicle to me.

Deirdre McDonnell was up to visit him and of course I had to break the news to him.

Faoi Ghlas

He told me some weeks later that the news spoiled his whole visit but then again, mine wasn't much good either.

When I come to think of it, I didn't have a lot of luck with comms or beartanna while in prison. While in the Crum in 1985, a non-political prisoner called McCullough was found hanging in his cell. He had been sentenced that day for his part in the murder of an elderly woman and after an altercation with the screws escorting him back from the courthouse, he had been placed in the punishment wing.

There was some concern regarding his treatment and Gerry had written a comm commenting on this. While Gerry was on a visit, the screws carried out a raid on our cell and the comm was recovered inside a book. The book had my name on it!

As a result, I received three days on the boards. While there I received a hard time from the screws. They told me the cell I was in, was the one where the hanging took place. I don't know if it was or not but I didn't sleep very soundly while there.

One of the people I most looked forward to seeing upon my arrival in the Blocks was Bobby Storey. I first met Bob Mór about 1979. Our first meeting was quite funny and when we are in company we vie with each other to see who will tell the story first.

It's normally Bobby as he's normally in charge!! Now it's my turn.

My nephew Patrick Adams was making his first communion in Matt Talbot Church which was about a quarter of a mile from my Mother's house on the Whiterock Road.

At this time there was a huge British army barracks overlooking the Whiterock Road and one of the spy posts had a clear view of the front door of our house.

Faoi Ghlas

In order to avoid being spotted by the Brit's my brothers had various ways in and out. One way was to enter by the front door of Anne Maguire's house, which was two doors up from our house, climb over her back fence and then over the fence of the house between our and her house. This led into our back garden and subsequently our back door.

We also had a huge metal fence surrounding our back garden and this ran alongside what was then the Michael Sloan's Club - a club named after a Fianna boy killed in 1972.

One of the bolts had been deliberately removed from the fence, this loosened the metal rail and left it easy to push this particular rail aside and enter through there. This entrance shielded you from the Brit spy post and was known to very few people.

The point I am making is that very few republicans entered our house by the front door.

Anyhow, to get back to the first meeting of me and Bob Mór.

I was busy watching television on the Saturday morning that Patrick made his communion when the doorbell rang. I opened the door and there was this giant of a man whom I had never saw before. He had thick black hair (hard to believe now I know!) and he continually looked over his shoulder at the Brit spy post.

After a few seconds he stammered out,

"Am, am, am, am, is P-P-P Paddy there?"

Now, unbeknown to Bobby, I also had a stammer! This was a reaction to the trauma I suffered as a six-year-old child after British soldiers fired CS gas into my bedroom.

Faoi Ghlas

No." I replied, "He is at-at-at Patrick's c-c-c communion."

"Whe-whe where is it? I-I-I am-am, I'm Bobby Sssss-storey and I need to-to see him n-n-now." The giant said to me.

The name rang a bell with me and as he stammered out some more I felt my anxiety worsen. The sweat was pouring over me and I could also see the anxiety on Bobby's face - he looked the way I was feeling!

After a couple of minutes and very little coherent conversation I let him in to the house. He was glad to be off the street and out of the way of the spy post and I was now feeling more confident that he was who he said he was.

We have become good friends since then and of course the more we tell the story the longer it gets! After that Bobby was a regular visitor to our house (now via the back door) and I would take great pride in running messages for him, Paddy and Big Marshall.

On one occasion about 1979, I was sent to tell people to vacate a house in Ballymurphy as an intercepted police message had reported a pending raid.

As I ran through the 'Murph, the familiar sound of Brit jeeps could be heard in the distance. I was panting for breath and my adrenalin was pumping as I reached the street. There were no Brits around as I ran up the path and hammered on the door.

Big Duice answered it but I could not, for the life of me get the words out!

"Am-am-am-am-am" was all I could say. I took a deep breath and tried again but all that came out of my mouth was an incoherent, "am-am-am-am-am".

Faoi Ghlas

I could imagine the Brits in the next street and I was literally doubled over trying to get the words out. By this stage Duice knew something was up and he grabbed me by the shoulders and shook me hard.

"What the fuck is it?" he shouted into my face.

And without a word of stammering I told him very clearly,

"Quick, get out. The Brits are coming."

In no time at all they were safely out and shortly after that the Brits raided the very house but were too late. Buiochas le Dia.

Duice was one of the first prisoners I met in 1986 and he laughed as he recalled my efforts to warn him.

Anyway back to Bobby. He arrived into our wing a couple of months after my own arrival. We soon got yarning. Over two nights we sat in his cell and he told me the story of the 1983 Escape from planning stages through to completion.

It was fascinating and I was awestruck by it. I know it's a cliché but if the Brits had have carried out this escape from Colditz they would still be making films on it. Bobby being Bobby commented later that it usually only took him one night to tell that story but with me it took two!

In November 1986 I was moved from H5 to H2 .I had expected to move as the prison administration operated a policy of moving prisoners from wing to wing and block to block. This was designed to disrupt us settling into a wing and becoming too familiar with the screws and workings of each block.

Some prisoners were moved every two or three weeks at a time. These people were known as 'Red Books'. The name was taken from the colour

Faoi Ghlas

of the book in which their every move was recorded by the screws. Their security classification was high risk and there was a whole sense of paranoia surrounding some of them from the screws.

I was fortunate enough to be moved on average about every seven or eight months. With a constant rate of moves on every wing it was about the right length of time to get to know most people. My cousin, Daithi was across the wing from me in H2 and I got to yarn with him every Sunday at Mass.

Jim Creighton was also there as was his brother, Axel, another wrongly accused person. Many people like Axel spent years in jail and were totally innocent of that they were accused off.

My first Christmas came and went in the Blocks. Geordie Murtagh was the entertainments officer and he organised a concert. I stayed well clear of it. When it comes to music, singing or acting I am talentless.

I remember New Year's Eve that year. It was one of those occasions when doing wack got the better of you. I was in bed well before midnight and had no enthusiasm for ringing out the old and bringing in the new. I longed to be outside with my family and not separated from them. Loneliness was biting in and I wished I were somewhere else. Thankfully I nodded off to sleep and woke in a better mood.

Early in 1986 we embarked upon a campaign to have H1 and H2 closed. We didn't openly declare we wanted the two blocks closed but instead we set upon a campaign of making the two blocks inoperable. The reason for wanting the two blocks closed cannot be revealed but it would have benefited republicans if we had all been held in the confines of H3 to H8.

Prisoners set about wrecking toilet bowls or sinks and causing electrical faults in the oven hot plates. As this happened they simultaneously

Faoi Ghlas

complained to the screws that these two blocks were not workable. When a Governor or Leine Bán came down the wings they were surrounded and bombarded with complaints.

On one occasion I was tasked to distract one of the screws while one of the boys set about wrecking a toilet bowl. As I stood talking to the screw and tried to steer him away from his position of being close to the toilet area there was this almighty smashing sound.

"What was that?" he said.

"What?" said I. "I didn't hear anything?"

Seconds later the comrade appears from the toilet area and with a total expression of innocence declares;

"Hey, that toilet bowl just collapsed!"

"Oh" said the screw. "Another one?"

No sooner was this toilet bowl replaced when another one would develop a leak or a crack would appear in a sink. In March of that year H2 was closed and we were divided round the other blocks but only two days later it was reopened and another group of republicans were moved into there.

Danny McGarrigle from Strabane and I were amongst this new group. We had both been part of the group involved in the initial campaign. The next day the Leine Bán in charge of the Block came down the wing. Danny and I immediately approached him and rhymed off the arguments and grievances we had over conditions in H2.

The following day the two of us were once again moved to different blocks.

Faoi Ghlas

It never ceased to amaze me how the administration believed that if they moved republicans they felt to be a nuisance that these republicans would suddenly stop being nuisances. As if a change of cell or change of wing would change your psyche.

This time I ended up in H8. While I was there, and during a conversation with a comrade, some of the reasoning behind the attempts to close H1 and H2 became clearer. Unfortunately, events did not materialise as planned and this will have to remain a story for another day.

In 1987 I got married to Ena. We had been going together at the time of my arrest and Ena visited me regularly. Against advice from almost everyone we decided to marry in the prison chapel. Within three years we were divorced. I have no bad feelings towards Ena. Ours was not the only relationship to crumble under the strain.

Also in 1987, the camp staff of the previous three years was replaced by a new staff. This new leadership had been to the fore during the Blanket protest and three of them were former hunger strikers. Their first task was to organize a campaign designed to improve our living conditions. Apart from this obvious intention, paramount in the thinking of the camp staff was the realisation, that with the turnover in prisoners, and with a lot of former blanketmen no longer in the jail, very few prisoners were experienced in jail struggle and how to campaign for certain issues.

In my own case, and I think it was similar to a lot of others, during my time in the Crum I had had no friction of any huge proportion with unionist prisoners or the prison administration. I was sentenced in 1986 to the H-Blocks where the conditions and 'freedom' afforded to republican prisoners had already been won by the sacrifices made in 1981 and through the segregation campaign of 1982. I believe there was perhaps a staleness creeping into newly and recently sentenced prisoners and the camp staff decided to stifle this.

Faoi Ghlas

Camp wide meetings were held and members of the camp staff who were on the 'red book' were able to use their status (albeit an unwanted status) to travel throughout the camp and promote issues relating to the campaign. Prisoners were invited to make suggestions as to how conditions could be improved. No suggestions were ruled out and none were considered too small or too big to be included.

Soon a large dossier of improvements had been drawn up and Leo Green presented this to the prison administration in his capacity as O.C. These improvements included issues such as a longer access to the canteen area, the provision of multi gyms, longer visiting hours and the abolition of the Red Book security categorisation. It also included the end to the policy of denying compassionate parole to some prisoners - this practice of denying a person's right to attend a family funeral was used in a most vindictive manner.

When one reflected on some of the issues, it was ridiculous that we were denied improvements that could only lead to a smoother running of the prison and lessen the potential for confrontation between republicans and the prison administration.

Campaign committees were established in every wing and a series of coordinated activities began. Selected prisoners requested to be allowed items such as a hat or scarf. These were previously disallowed to us, and when they were again refused, the prisoner set about the process of taking the issue to a higher level within the administration.

Each week we sought something different and soon the momentum increased. A new approach to challenging governors on our wings was also introduced. Previous to this, if a governor came onto our wings to 'inspect' the running of the place we would gather round him in a large crowd and barrack him. Now it was left to one or two selected people to approach them and calmly discuss the conditions situation. If the

Faoi Ghlas

opportunity arose to isolate the governor and get him alone, it was quietly pointed out to him that we were not just a group of prisoners seeking improvements in isolation from the outside world. He was reminded that we had the support of many people outside and that support had backed us before.

This had the desired affect and soon the governors were claiming that improvements were outside of their remit and the people we needed to talk to were the Northern Ireland Office itself. This was fine and I don't

Three of my nieces, Maura, Áine and Sinéad on the occasion of their First Communion circa 1990.

think negotiating with such people frightened the camp staff.

Faoi Ghlas

After a period of time it was decided to up the ante a bit. It was the practice that prisoners were locked in their cells from 12.30 to 2pm in order to facilitate the screws lunch period. Two prisoners were permitted to stay in the wing canteen over this period. They were locked in, in much the same manner as those prisoners locked in their cells and indeed the wing itself where we were held, was also locked. We argued that more, if not all prisoners should be able to avail of the opportunity to stay in the canteen over the lunch period. This of course was denied to us.

Chris Moran was the O.C. on our wing in H7 at this time (1988) and it was decided that four of us would stay out in the canteen over this period. This was replicated throughout the prison in every republican wing. Just before lunchtime lock-up, each wing O.C. approached the screws in their wings and informed them that four republican prisoners would be refusing to lock up over this period and that they would remain in the canteen. It was stressed that the protest was to be peaceful and any attempts by prison riot squads to remove us would be met with peaceful resistance.

The four chosen to stay out in our wing were Chris as the O.C. along with Kevin McCallion, Scotchie Kearney and myself. We had no idea how the prison administration would react to this and so we waited in the canteen in anticipation. Soon enough a léine bán appeared at the canteen gate and told us we were breaking prison rules and were liable to disciplinary measures. Chris explained our position as outlined, the léine bán noted it and left, and that was that.

At 2pm we were unlocked and life continued as normal. A total anti-climax!

The following day we were informed that we were to be charged and appear in front of a governor for adjudication. The scéal had reached our

Faoi Ghlas

wing via the visits that other republicans had already appeared in front of these 'courts' and had been found two weeks 'loss of privileges' suspended for a period of three months. When it came our turn we were each called out to see the governor in the circle. I was amused when the governor turned out to be the same Crumlin Road governor, Smith. I noted from his demeanor that he also recognised me from previous encounters.

I had a prepared reply to the charges rhymed off to a tee in my head and the first chance I got I rattled it off. I had been nervous due to my stammer and the prospect of getting tongue-tied in front of screws was bothering me. When I spoke, the words flowed out minus the stammer and as I pumped my chest out in celebration of this, Smith informed me that I would have to repeat my speech for the benefit of the court minutes. BASTARD!!! I could see the glee in his eyes.

This time the words came out slower but the message was the same.

Another development in the conditions campaign was the Red Book issue. We had decided that the next time a Red Book prisoner was informed that he was to move that he would refuse to do so. When this came around, the first two moves concerned our wing. Martin Meehan was informed that he was moving from our wing to another block and that his place on our wing was to be taken by Gerry Kelly.

Along with the wing O.C. Martin told the administration that he would be refusing the move. We were informed that afternoon that the riot squad would come in and move Martin after the 8.30pm lock up. Negotiations continued with the camp staff and the administration throughout the day but shortly after 8.30 lock up, the riot squad arrived in.

Faoi Ghlas

Ten or twelve of them proceeded down the wing to Martin's cell as we watched out the sides of our cell doors. The riot squad was dressed in overalls with protective padding, gloves, helmets and visors pulled down concealing their identities. Martin's cell door was opened and the sound of the heavy bolt being shot forward into place echoed throughout the wing. This was immediately followed by the sound of rushing footsteps and the groans and pants of the screws as they surrounded Martin and forced him on to the cell floor.

When this was completed, and Martin was motionless, he was lifted by his two arms and legs and while one screw held his head in a downward position, he was carried from the wing onto the next block. We banged our doors in support of Martin and shouts of 'Up the 'Ra' and 'Go ahead Martin' accompanied him as he passed our cells but in reality, locked behind our doors, we were helpless.

Minutes later Gerry Kelly arrived onto the wing - he was carried in much the same manner as Martin. As he was carried down the wing to his cell he was greeted with more shouts of encouragement from the rest of us. He recounted the next day that when the screws reached his cell and after putting him face down on the floor, they literally run out the door as fast they could and slammed it shut.

More Red Book moves followed in other republican wings on the days after this and these led to a deterioration in relations between the prison administration and us. The ordinary run of the mill screw went out of his way to let us know that they were not members of the riot squad and in fact had no problems in the notion of republicans gaining improvements in their living conditions.

In October 1988 just before we were unlocked, we heard on the 2pm radio news that a prison officer based in the H-Blocks had been blown up and killed in an undercar booby trap explosion.

Faoi Ghlas

As we left our cells and walked onto the wings it was clear the screws were aware of what had happened and this showed in their approach to us. I began a conversation with one in the hope of finding out who had died. He told me it was Brian Armour, a leading member of the Prison Officer's Association (P.O.A).

Two or three days later the P.O.A. called their members out on strike to coincide with the funeral of Brian Armour. As a result of this we were locked in our cells throughout the day and denied access to canteen and toilet facilities.

It also meant that RUC personnel were brought into the camp to oversee the running of the prison. Their lack of prison experience was fully illustrated when it came to the 'packed lunches' that were handed out to us as a way of a meal.

One of the most important possessions for any republican prisoner was stretch and seal cling film. We used cling film to seal our comms and beartanna and anything else we needed to conceal upon ourselves.

It was probably the most used commodity in the camp and was always in demand. So imagine our delight when the Peelers handed us sandwiches and all sorts of food wrapped in swathes of stretch and seal.

It was Christmas come early! We had supplies to last for months, courtesy of the RUC!!!

I found screws strange beings. No doubt some of them treated their job as just that - a job! Others I believed did not have the courage to join the RUC or loyalist paramilitaries to fight the IRA, and hoped their role in imprisoning republicans would suffice for this. Some were easy to manipulate. This was generally achieved by striking up a rapport with individual screws and over a period of time building up a relationship with them. This 'relationship' with certain screws was beneficial when it

Faoi Ghlas

came to smuggling on visits. If a screw with whom you had a rapport happened to be your escort, he would generally leave you alone.

Some screws were clearly loyalists and rebuffed any approach by republicans at small chat. Still, day in and day out selected groups of republicans made it their business to engage with the screws.

The screws consistently backstabbed their colleagues and their bosses. Their main motivation was money and the huge financial incentives their job rewarded them. Their disloyalty was obvious.

Some of them were incredibly naive. Within weeks of a new screw arriving into our wings he would break every rule handed down to him by the prison administration. On one occasion, Scamall Dubh and another comrade noticed that this particular screw wore his coat down onto the wing and would leave it in the screw's office. The office was very rarely occupied and the two prisoners decided to act.

The next day, seconds after the screw had left his coat in the office and headed off to the top gate, the comrade entered the office and proceeded to search through the coat pockets. Scamall Dubh kept him occupied while the comrade copied down the screw's driving licence details onto a cigarette paper.

Suddenly he heard the screw being summoned out to the circle. As Scamall Dubh tried to delay the screw getting back to the office for his coat, our comrade had no time to put the licence back and so stuffed it down the front of his jeans.

The screw entered the office as our comrade pretended to be looking for clothes collection forms, lifted his coat and walked out to the circle. The two prisoners were now in possession of the licence but it was not an ideal situation. As they toyed with the idea of leaving it on the office floor by way it had fallen from the pocket the screw returned.

Faoi Ghlas

Straight down the wing he walked, took his coat off and left it in its usual position. In no time at all the licence was returned to the coat pocket and the screw wasn't any the wiser.

Conditions throughout the camp were still improving. Red Book prisoners were remaining on wings for longer periods, parole for republicans was becoming more available (though Red Book prisoners were still victimised when it came to this) and we were getting our heads round the issue of Lifer releases.

A life-sentenced prisoner had his case for release 'reviewed' by the Life Sentence Review Board after ten years and were often 'knocked back' for up to five years before his or her case was heard again.

Republicans began to challenge this route to release and began to expose the inadequacies of the system. This led to a light at the end of the tunnel for prisoners and their families. One could sense a good deal of confidence among republican prisoners and this was reinforced as we gained more improvements to our living conditions.

It was around this time also that the media reported that an escape plan had been foiled. Very few of us were aware of this but it did lead to a screw appearing in court on charges related to it. It also led to raids by screws and the RUC and two stories spring to mind.

I was fairly handy with the needle and thread and the odd time I would be asked to turn up a pair of jeans by one of the boys. On this occasion the sewing lasted until 2am and just as I was turning off my cell light I noticed four white clad figures walking up the yard towards the entrance to the block. I rushed to the window and caught another glimpse of them just before they went out of view. They were dressed totally in white from head to toe and were obviously forensic peelers.

Faoi Ghlas

Lorney McKeown was across from me on the other side of the wing and as a member of the camp staff, he was sure to be carrying beartanna. I got up to the side of my door and shouted across to Lorney.

"Lorney, Lorney, an bhfuil tú ag éisteach liom?" ("Are you listening to me?")

After several attempts he finally woke and called back to me.

"Cad é?" ("What?").

"Sílim go bhfuil an cuardach isteach." ("I think the search team is in").

Lorney, sleep all over his voice replied.

" An bhfuil tú cinnte?" (Are you sure?")

The shouting alerted others and soon the wing was alive with the sound of pipes being rattled and comrades being alerted to the possibility of a raid. Fifteen minutes passed and there was no sound of movement whatsoever from the direction of the circle. Someone called out to ask me was I sure I had seen someone. Yes, I was sure but after another fifteen minutes (which seemed like fifteen hours) I began to doubt myself. What if I had been too tired and imagined it? I was beginning to picture the abuse and slagging I would receive the next morning if I had woken the whole wing by mistake when Lorney called out to me:

"Dominic, an bhfuil aon rud eile ann?" (Is there anything else?).

As I was about to answer him, the sound of the wing gate being unlocked brought me to the gap at the side of the door. I looked up but was unable to see anything. Then one of the boys in a cell near the top of the wing shouted out that a search team was in the multi-gym. Talk about relief!! I was never as glad to see a search team!

Faoi Ghlas

It transpired that an RUC forensics team had come in and carried out a forensic examination of the multi-gym area. Next morning, I was able to eat my breakfast safe in the knowledge that I wasn't going mad and had saved the wing from a potential surprise raid.

The second story, which springs to mind, involves (Seosamh 'An Fear Gault'). Seos is one of the funniest men I have ever met and he wound me up at every opportunity. On this occasion the screws raiding party entered the wing in the early hours of the morning and systematically searched each cell.

Seos was in the next cell to me. He woke me from my sleep to alert me to the raid. I rose quickly, and having learned my lesson regarding bearteanna I quickly concealed the one I was carrying and pulled on a pair of shorts. In no time, the screws were in Seos's cell and I watched out the side of my door as he was led from his own cell and put into the big cell while a raid on his own was carried out.

I was next and the same procedure was carried out. No problems I thought as I returned to the cell afterwards and proceeded to tidy the place up a bit. It was then I heard the screws back at Seos's cell and so I immediately returned to the gap at the side of the door to see what was happening. I caught a glimpse of Seos going back into the big cell and I could hear the screws rummage through his cell again.

Minutes later they came out and I could see from their faces they weren't at all happy. Seos was brought back to his cell. He walked in that inimitable style; hands behind his back and eyes looking upwards. There was guilt written all over his face -I was well aware of this stance having experienced his messing on numerous occasions.

The next morning, I discovered that the raiding party had left behind them (in Seos's cell) a document outlining the search and the names of

Faoi Ghlas

the screws involved therein. When Seos returned to his cell after the first raid and subsequently noticed the screws mistake, he immediately returned the said document to them...did he heck! Rather he bangled it (concealed it on his person). When the screws returned to the cell the second time and Seos was brought to the big cell, he immediately gave it to the next prisoner and thus the document was lost to the screws.

Seos tortured me but I lapped him up. For some reason or another if I moved onto a wing he always followed me within days and likewise if he moved, I followed - and worse - we constantly ended up within cells of each other.

On the locker in my cell sat a Malteser box, which I used for storing pens, stamps and batteries etc. (I used to eat Malteser sweets by the box load). On three or four consecutive nights I opened the box to take out a pen and there in the box lay a dead wasp. This mystified me.

One-day walking around the yard with Seos, he diverted the conversation to a discussion of our favourite chocolates. (And there was you thinking that republican prisoners discussed the writings of Marx and Lenin!). I immediately thought of the Maltesers and the wasps and began to tell him of my discovery.

He told me, without any sign of a reddner that his sister also stored her pens in a Malteser box and the honey from the Maltesers attracted the wasps. I bought it hook, line and sinker!! Next night I found another wasp and I can still see myself now smelling the box for honey as I peered into it. Days later Seos broke and told me that he had been putting the wasps into the box all along. I swear I hated him. Never crossed my mind however to query how the wasps opened the box, climbed inside and closed it behind them!

Faoi Ghlas

Seos took great delight in coming between me and Maltesers. During the winter nights when the exercise yards were closed, groups of us would head off to some-one's cell, open a packet of biscuits and soon the craic would start. Someone would tell a story and this would be bettered by another and so on until at times you might have nine or ten people crowded into a cell. Sometimes Digger or Tomboy would pull out the guitar or mandolin and a sing-song would ensue.

On this occasion it was nearing New Year's Eve and Seos was aware I had a box of Maltesers stashed in my clothes locker. I had stupidly told him while walking round the yard the previous day- yes I know I should have known better! My plan was to scoff them down as it neared midnight on the 31st. I know others celebrate the New Year with champagne but Maltesers would have to do me.

This particular night as a group of us sat spoofing in the cell I hadn't noticed Seos slipping out for a minute or two. Shortly after he returned to the cell he produced a box of Maltesers and began to pass them round us all. When the box was finished, which didn't take long, he gleefully announced where they had come from!

As the years passed I trained vigorously and worked hard at staying fit. I loved soccer and the opportunities we got to play it in the Blocks. At least once a week we went to the 'Big Pitch' - an eleven-a-side football pitch. Here the rivalry between the teams was unreal. Lots of people, me included, became demons once they crossed the white line. Winning was all important and those who didn't take it as serious as us probably thought we were all mad.

Despite the best efforts of the prison administration it was fairly easy to work out when the Block you were in was next due to play on the pitch. For hours on end we would draw up the team and the formation. Dessie Collins worked on his team for days.

Faoi Ghlas

A minimum of twenty people were required to go to the pitch or your Block had to forfeit its turn. Some blocks had no problems getting twenty-two people - others found it more difficult. We normally played one wing against the other and whoever won had bragging rights until the next game.

If you ended up with lots of footballers on a block it was not unusual to hope you would have access to the pitch when the other wing's best players would have their visits!

On the other hand, if you were in a block where it was difficult to get twenty-two players, some non-footballers would offer to go down and 'play'. In reality they were making the numbers up and of course it was the comradely thing to do to ensure that your block did not lose the opportunity to play.

Fra Gormley was one such man. From Middletown in Armagh he knew more about milking cows than he did kicking footballs. Fra idolised Graeme Sharpe who then played for Everton. One day, after Fra missed a sitter in front of the net I nicknamed him 'Fra Blunt'. Other comrades (Rab Kerr springs to mind) literally stood in the centre circle and spoke to each other.

If the ball went near them they got out of the way of it.

Skeet said they were like the moving statues at Ballinspittle. (Around this time, people in Ballinspittle in rural Ireland had claimed to witness statues moving).

There were some brilliant players and one wonders what would have become of Meaders, Paul Baker, Leonard Fenin, Eddie Harkin and suchlike if the war had not impacted upon their lives. Brian Campbell was the hardest player I ever played against. He was so strong and seemed to be everywhere on the pitch. Tomboy was a smashing goal

Faoi Ghlas

keeper and he and I had some duels. He would tell me before a match that I wouldn't score past him. As the match went on and I didn't score I would get more anxious and he more confident.

Most times, however, I would just score early and have it out of the way!!

On one occasion a match turned into a mass brawl and the camp staff banned our block from playing wing against wing until we caught ourselves on.

The other wing had won the previous six or seven matches and was fairly rubbing into us the fact they were better and would wind us up by offering us some of their players. Invariably these players were their weaker players. We refused to bow down and would go to the pitch, knowing a thrashing awaited us, before agreeing to mix the teams.

Over a period of several weeks the personnel on the wings changed. Some of their better players were moved to other blocks and in turn we were getting good players on to our wing. The score line by which the other wing won was starting to decrease in line with this. In one match we gained a draw and the other wing knew the game was up.

Over the next week more footballers moved onto our wing while the other wings resources depleted further. We were confident of victory and let them know this!

The time arrived and we kicked off. Five minutes into the game Wee Teapot was tackled by Big Jazz. Teapot is no slouch but he's only three-quarters the size of Jazz. They both squared up to each other. If truth be told it was handbags stuff and before anything could transpire some of us were in between them.

Faoi Ghlas

I thought it was settled but suddenly out of nowhere Tomboy appeared in the defence of Teapot and he and Jazz began wrestling on the ground. Bik jumped in and tried to break it up but only succeeded in receiving a blow below his eye which needed stitches.

It was bedlam for several minutes before order was restored. Inevitably the story was soon doing the rounds of the other blocks and our block O.C. received a teac' from the Camp Staff telling us to desist from inter-wing matches for a while.

On only one occasion did I feel like hitting anyone on the pitch and he was a screw! On occasions if you went to the pitch with twenty-one players the screw who normally refereed the match would play so as to make the numbers up. During a match I was put through in a one-against-one with a screw. I was fairly quick then and as I knocked the ball past him and attempted to run on he stuck his leg out and knocked me flying. I was raging though it was probably more to do with it being a screw than anything else.

I got up off the ground and made for him. Luckily Raymond McCartney stepped in and calmed me down. To be fair to the screw, a man called Billy Traynor, he apologised and said I was too fast for him.

During one game I was tackled by Pat Masterson. He struck me in the stomach with his knee and I went down. The pain was unbearable and I had to go off. That night there was blood in my urine and I went to the doctor. He told me I had bruised my kidneys and to do no physical training for four weeks. The thought of this was doing my head in as I trained in some shape or form at least once a day.

After two weeks I had had enough and took part in a light weights session in the multi-gym. Everything seemed fine for about two hours and then over the 12.30 to 2pm lock-up I began to experience the most

Faoi Ghlas

severe pains. I thought I was having a heart attack though I didn't know how a heart attack should feel! I resisted the urge to ring the alarm bell and seek help - for some reason the idea of it didn't appeal to me. After an hour the pains eased and I visited the doctor again. He told me off for not following his advice and then barred me from physical activity for another four weeks. Served me right!

I also had the misfortune of spending a night in the prison hospital after Pat Wilson tackled me during another match. Not only did he tackle me but as I fell, he also fell, and landed on my ankle just as it twisted. I was on crutches for a fortnight with torn ligaments.

That night while in the hospital I asked the medical officer on duty did he know which of the ten hunger strikers had died in the cell in which I was to be sleeping? He didn't know!!

I had a sound sleep anyhow and was privileged to share the same space as one of the Ten.

Having said all of that about the big pitch, the vast majority of games were played in great spirits and any animosity was left on the pitch once the game ended. Only those of us who shared the craic of the Big Pitch will understand the escapism it provided for us - years after I was released republican prisoners were able to play inter-block matches and a formal league was established -I can just imagine the competition!!

In October 1989, prison caught up with Our Sean. An active republican from his early teens he had many close shaves but always came out the right side of them but not this time. That Saturday afternoon news bulletins had been reporting several shooting attacks by the Army in Belfast that day and there was press speculation of an attempted break out from the Crum. That night it was reported that two men had been arrested after a shooting in Ballymurphy. Sinn Fein, in a statement, said

Faoi Ghlas

that both men had received severe beatings from the RUC during their arrest.

We had no way of receiving sceál as to who it was until the next visiting day which was the following Tuesday. Then when my mother arrived up she told me that Sean and a former Divismore Park neighbour of our family, Anthony Gillen, had been the two arrested. Her heart was breaking but she was as strong as ever as she told me that in all likelihood they would both be charged. Several days later Sean and Anthony were indeed charged with possession of an AK47 Assault Rifle.

I knew that Sean was a fairly active republican and that this situation would arise sooner or later but I took consolation from the fact he wasn't dead.

I thought of the deaths of Big Dan McCann, Sean Savage and Mairéad Farrell in Gibraltar and how the time between receiving such sceál via the radio and the next visit was the most unbearable time.

The midnight news at the time of the Gibraltar shootings carried an Army statement that all three people killed were from Belfast and their names would be released once their families were notified. I don't think very many of us slept that night.

On the 7 O'clock news the following morning I heard the names. Big Dan I knew well and I was often in the company of Sean Savage in the months prior to my arrest. Mairéad, I knew off from her days on hunger strike in 1980.

Again we heard the sceál of their funerals being attacked on the radio: the first reports suggested a mortar attack and many casualties. I was

Faoi Ghlas

locked in my cell when Radio Ulster interrupted its programme to go live to Milltown Cemetery.

I lay on the bed feeling totally helpless. It's impossible to describe the feeling of total inadequacy. I am not suggesting I would have or could have influenced events had I been outside but in a prison cell, behind a locked door, I was no use to anyone - totally powerless. I feared for my family and friends and for the mourners.

My family was sure to be there. (Two of my nephews, Eamonn McCaughley and Patrick Mulvenna was injured in the attack). When I watched the television that night I was amazed at the bravery of the many people who ran at the attacker as opposed to away from him. Their bravery saved many lives but unfortunately three people died including another Army Volunteer, Caoimhin Mac Brádaigh.

I can remember the total frustration we experienced as we watched other funerals being attacked and people being harassed by the RUC as they tried to bury their dead. On the outside people were able to do something: protest, riot, join the 'RA and attend the funerals. All we could do was watch news after news after news.

For us it was also a tense period. Frustrated by our inability to contribute to outside events we could only view from afar. The ten miles from Belfast to Long Kesh may well have been ten million miles.

The scéal I got from my visits never conveyed the full story. My family, not wishing to concern me more, were hesitant in what they told me and thus I have always felt a detachment from those terrible events of March 1988.

By August 1989 I had completed my fifth year of imprisonment - nothing in comparison to some of the lengths that some prisoners had served but five years nevertheless. I remember wakening up one morning and

Faoi Ghlas

thinking to myself: Jesus, Dominic in two years you'll be out of here! I had to repeat this for it to sink in.

I was also approaching my GCE Irish language O level exam. This I passed with a Grade A and was well pleased. I also obtained a Fáinne Óir which equaled a proficient fluency leis an teanga féin. Go raibh maith agat a Sheamais don obair mhaith a rinne tu liomsa.

It was round this time I received severe burns due to an accident with hot water. The administration had supplied us with an eight inch deep wire basket. About two feet by three feet in rectangular shape it served as a strainer into which we placed washed dishes and dipped them into a steriliser unit. The lid of the strainer would not close properly and had the potential to scald the user if the water overflowed. I had notified Kevin McCallion of this. Kevin dealt with the screws in relation to such matters and he in turn had notified the screws several times.

One day I was washing the dishes with Adrian Kelly and as I lifted the cage from the steriliser a bowl full of hot water dislodged itself. I could see it happening but was unable to get the basket away from me. The water came out of the basket and down my groin, upper right thigh and my right foot. It was summer time and fortunately all I was wearing was a pair of football shorts. I immediately stripped them off me and run to the cold water tops at the top of the wing.

There I splashed myself with water and after wrapping myself in a towel I made my way out to the medical officer. There I was treated and the next day the doctor informed me I had second degree burns.

After a while I made a claim for compensation. The administration contested the claim on the grounds that my refusal to accept instruction in the use of the basket contributed to my injuries. We managed to prove in court that no records of offered instructions from the

Faoi Ghlas

administration existed, to which the administration countered that we would not have accepted such instructions anyway, as we were republicans and took care of proceedings on our own wings.

Kevin and Adrian both gave their accounts of what happened as I did myself. The judge, in his wisdom, awarded me compensation for my injuries but proceeded to immediately slash the award in half ......because we 'refused instruction'. Good old British justice!

Our time in the Crum and Long Kesh was always brightened up by some unfortunate comrade falling victim to a slip of the tongue or a spoonerism where the brain worked slower than the tongue (or perhaps didn't work at all). I must admit I was fond of the odd spoonerism myself.

Once, while walking in the yard with Foxy Callan from Derry I remarked, during a discussion on Sinn Féin's relationship with other parties, that we needed to extend the friend of handship to the SDLP. I meant hand of friendship of course!

On another occasion I received a letter from an Australian woman. When asked by a comrade who it was, I replied, "Ach just some Australian woman from America". It's beyond me how it came out as it did but it did!

Tonkas Moran from Turf Lodge was susceptible to the frequent mishap also when it came to the Queen's English. Once at a meeting in the big cell he declared that when he got out he was going to touch for 'a bird' and to hell with what people still in jail thought. Life outside jail was different and that's how it was he announced unashamedly.

"A bird?" said Spike who was chairing the meeting.

Faoi Ghlas

"Well ok, birds" Tonkas said, completely missing the point of Spike's admonishment.

Lorney McKeown constantly encouraged people to read and one particular book he promoted was entitled 'Dialectical Materialism'. A chapter in the book carried the title 'Mechanistic Materialism'. One of the boys was heard to say that he couldn't make head nor tail of it and with absolutely no pun intended continued to describe the book as a 'load of hydraulics'.

One night we were holding a quiz. Winter nights always evoked an idea in some person's mind to do something by way of entertainment. Most of us were happy to watch T. V. or take part in ranganna but not everyone.

Bap McGreavey was the Quizmaster on this occasion.

"Which famous film maker made 54 cartoons?"

His question was met with a stunned silence. Say it again Bap someone said. "Which famous film maker made 54 cartoons?" Total silence!

Bap showed the question to his fellow quizmaster who re-read the question...

"Which famous film maker made 54 cartoons?" The answer of course was Walt Disney.

Back to Tonkas: one night his wing commune was bereft of coffee. Tonkas sauntered up to the grills dividing his wing from the other wing. Spotting a comrade on the landing opposite Tonkas called out,

"Mo chara, have you's any coffee to the shop arrives tomorrow?"

Faoi Ghlas

The comrade answered, "Aye how much do you want?"

"Enough for a cup of tea" said Tonkas.

Now lest Tonkas thinks I am picking on him and leaving others alone I will tell the tale of the biggest verbal mishap in the history of Long Kesh and the culprit was my good self!

One winter night about ten thirty or so, the most horrendous shower of rain arrived over our block. It was coming down in buckets and the noise it made as it bounced three feet off the ground was deafening. It was so loud that I closed my cell window. I rarely did this as I preferred a flow of fresh air when sleeping.

Now just a short while before the rain had begun a comrade had been playing his radio a bit too loud for the liking of Brendan 'Bleep' Mailey.

Bleep didn't like to be disturbed at the best of times and the fact he had to get up to his door from the horizontal position he was used to on his bed obviously annoyed him further. Eventually after three or four shouts of 'turn that radio down' followed by a more aggressive 'turn that fucking radio down' silence descended on the wing.

When I woke the next morning the events of the night before were still on my mind. Rain, radio, noise 'turn it off', closed window etc. Still half asleep I crawled out of bed, made my way past the early morning joggers and sat down next to Digger McCrory at the breakfast table and poured myself a bowl of cornflakes.

"Did you hear the rain last night?" said Digger.

"Aye" said I in reply, and for some unexplainable reason I finished my sentence with...

Faoi Ghlas

"I had to get up and turn it off."

I can still see Digger's face as he looked at me as if I was nuts before he erupted in a fit of laughter. The funny thing is I knew I was saying it. It was almost like I could hear what I said before the words came out of my mouth but I still said them. Mad, but as I said, unexplainable.

Rinty McVeigh was another character, a real wit. Rab Kerr on the other hand was a big serious man. Rinty found out that Rab was learning German and suggested to Rab that they share a cell over lock-up and practice their German.

Rab readily agreed and arrangements were made.

When Rinty entered Rab's cell, he found Rab had the books laid out and the tea and biscuits sorted - everything was ready for a heavy session.

"Right Rinty, go ahead, you start," said Rab.

Rinty smiled, put on his best German accent and said,

"Vat is your name and Ver do you live?"

Rab was fuming!

Needless to say they spent the next 45 minutes in total silence but the minute the cell was opened Rinty was out like a shot and relayed the story to everyone he met.

The last mishap I will give to our Sean.

A lot of the boys would use slang like 'fork and knife' for wife and other such phrases. Sean wasn't as fluent in this manner of speaking as some

Faoi Ghlas

of them and lo and behold he returned from a visit with a beaming smile and on a high from his exertions.

"Well, Sean had you a good visit? Who was up?" came the usual questions as he entered the yard and joined in the last lap with the last stragglers before lock-up.

"Ach you know the score" said Sean. "The knife and fork was up and I got an oul kuss and a ciddle."

As the stragglers rolled on the ground laughing all Sean could say was'

"Well fuck me, if all you's can use that oul slang so can I!!!"

Nicknames were another familiar trait in jail. I was known as Addies by my former school friends on the outside but while inside it was always Dominic. Unfortunately, that can't be said for others. Names such as Shammy, Skeet, Dikel, Bleep, Wuzz, Sweety Jar, Rinty, Ginty, Pickles, Sleepy, Crab, Scope, Scobie, Hatchet, Jackdaw, Cypie, Teapot, Flash, Meatman, Scoldy, Bunty, Greek, Jaz, Scamall Dubh, The Badger, Beaver, Nobby, Chopper, Buck, Cheeser, Abdul, Crip, Snooge, Dinker, Chinky, Beef, Jazz, Tonkas and Duice were heard day in and day out.

Now not all of these were probably politically correct but my favourite is Wooly Jumper also known as Martin Bullock from Tyrone.

I have a book at home 'Falls In Focus'. A compilation of photos taken in West Belfast in the 1980s, my mother sent it into me in September 1987. I carried it round with me for the following four years and every prisoner I served time with signed it. Looking over it now I am saddened by the number of people who have passed away. Ta siad ar bhothar an fhirinne anois.

Faoi Ghlas

People such as Harry McCavana, Seany Bateson, Spud Murphy, Big Ned Maguire, Colly Marks who died on active service. There are plenty of others. Big Duice who good naturedly slagged me about my stutter and Brian Campbell too. More recently we have lost Tony Catney, Mickey 'Beak' Holden, Jim Gillen and my old cell-mate Smitty from Fermanagh among many others.

May they all rest in peace.

While in the Blocks we were kept apart from republican prisoners who were still being held in the Cages. This was the name given to the section of Long Kesh where republicans arrested before March 1976 were held. There was the odd chance that a prisoner from the Blocks could meet one up with one of them while at the dentist or hospital as they sat in the waiting room.

One day I was in the waiting room when in walked Alec Crowe.

Alec had been imprisoned in the early 70s and had been held in the Cages ever since - he was a good friend of our family. Once when I was about five or six, I was very sick and began to throw up blood. My mother run out to the street to see if any neighbours could help. The first person she came across was Alec. He was driving an IRA patrol car with two or three other Volunteers all armed to the teeth with rifles.

Alec immediately lifted me into the car and I was delivered to the hospital courtesy of the IRA.

When Alec entered the dentist waiting room we instantly recognised each other and threw our arms round one another. He had always called me son when I was a child and he continued this while we spoke. Unfortunately I was soon brought back to the wing and we had to part.

Faoi Ghlas

On the way back the escorting screw asked me how I coped with my "father" in the Cages and me in the Blocks. Alec called me 'son' so many times the screw thought he was my father. Alec also died several years ago.

Martin Meehan is another who has left this world. Meehan was renowned as one of those who did his time while mixing and winding others up. He had only just been sentenced and arrived into our wing about 1986 or '87 and that night we walked the yard together. When he found out I had a visit the next day he asked me would I bring a greeting card out to my 'Da' as he knew him very well and they were good friends. Of course I agreed and early next morning Martin arrived in to my cell with the card. There were two or three others in the cell as Martin announced his arrival.

"Here Mo Chara, give that to your Da' and tell him his oul mate was asking, and your mummy too".

I looked down at the card to see it was addressed to 'Paddy and Anne-Marie Adams'. He thought I was our Paddy's son!!

His face lit up when I told him his mistake. The other two boys immediately ran out to tell the rest of the wing that Martin had messed up. He was raging but the look on his face was hilarious.

Several days later I was called out to the Circle and informed I had won a trip to Miami in a ballot drawn in St John's GAA club. I told the screw it was no good to me but I would try to get it passed on to one of my family. Martin had set the screw up to tell me this. I returned to the wing and relayed my disappointment at not getting to Miami to Billy Gorman. No sooner had I told Billy when Martin came running, whooping and shouting into the canteen in joy at catching me out. I tried to bluff I knew all along but was just wasting my time.

Faoi Ghlas

When Martin died in November 2007, several of us had the privilege of providing a Guard of Honour at his wake. Johnny Doc, Seany A' and Dikel were among those present. We spent the afternoon recalling Martin's exploits and to be honest he was probably laughing along with us.

Sometimes prison, and the long time some of us spent there took its toll on us. Some comrades suffered mental breakdowns. Years of stress and anguish, along with the brutality inflicted on some, and the lack of proper medical attention provided for those in that situation was a huge source of discontentment to us. The O.C. and his staff lobbied the administration on the issue but improvements were unsatisfactory.

On one occasion, a comrade lost total control of his mind. In all honesty, it was the most frightening time I spent in jail. An hour or so after 8.30pm lock-up, I heard a bit of commotion and several shouts.

I immediately turned the radio off and got up closer to the door to listen. Our comrade was in disarray. In his mind he believed there was someone or something in his cell. The hairs stood straight and tall on my neck as I heard him scream at the top of his voice:

"They're coming in the window."

The screaming was coming from the other wing but in the quietness and still of the night it was clearly audible. Some comrades were trying to speak to the unfortunate man and calm him down but it was having no affect.

After what seemed like an age the screw on night duty arrived but had to send out to the emergency control room for permission to open the cell door. Meanwhile our comrade's mind wandered further. His screaming intensified, our anxieties also intensified as did our frustration at being unable to help him.

Faoi Ghlas

Eventually access was made to his cell and he was transferred to the prison hospital.

I found it difficult to settle that night. The screams echoed in my mind and I lay awake for a long time. The next morning the O.C. enquired of our comrade and was informed he was in the prison hospital.

Others were not so fortunate. Paul Nugent was a young man from the Falls Road. His father was a republican and when Paul arrived in the Blocks for assaulting an RUC man, we took him under our direction. Though not a republican activist, Paul lived in our wings and behaved throughout his time there as one of us. Paul was an amateur boxer and spent most of his time practicing on a punch bag he had constructed from an old mattress. Each time he punched the bag Paul made the sound shoo.

Punch, Punch, shoo, shoo was a familiar sound when Paul was training in his cell.

One day I returned from a visit to be told by Rab Kerr that Paul, or Beaver, as he was better known had been found hanging in the prison hospital the previous night.

Christmas 1989 arrived and the Administration relaxed the rules regarding parole. More prisoners were now eligible and for those who qualified it was a great opportunity to spend time outside with their families. Red Book prisoners were still exempt from parole however. Pickles was one of these and happened to be on our wing at this particular time. I remember feeling sorry for him but fortunately this silly rule was changed soon after and those Red Books were soon able to taste some life on the outside.

My chance came in August 1990 as I entered my last year. I took two days parole.

Faoi Ghlas

They passed in a flash.

The night before I was due to return to the jail I went to the Felon's Club. Recently released Gerry Kelly was there. He tried to persuade me to go to the Féile in Springhill with him but I declined. I didn't want to be late back to the Blocks!! Tales of people going to the Féile in Springhill and disappearing for days were not unheard off!

Shortly after my return to the Blocks from parole, our Sean was sentenced to 14 years and soon he landed on our wing. Joe O'Neill from Turf Lodge was there too and for the next several weeks we had good craic together.

As 1990 became 1991 the time I had left to serve was measured in months. Marty Lynch used to say that right down to his last few weeks he tried to tell himself he had 'under two years' left as this took his mind off the 'Gate Fever'. I tried - it didn't work!

At Easter I took a weeks parole - it was to be my last before my release. On Easter Sunday I attended the parade along the Falls Road. My sister Anne and I walked back along the Falls Road afterwards and turned into Beechmount Avenue.

As we did so two RUC landrovers drew alongside us. Several heavily armed RUC personnel climbed out and surrounded us. I was shocked when the first one approached me and called me by my first name.

I was mystified as to how he knew me as prior to my arrest in 1984 I was relatively unknown to the Brits and RUC and was very rarely stopped in the street by them. Two others joined in and one told me that the last time he saw me I was laying cuffed at the side of the road. It dawned on me that some of them were obviously involved in my arrest. I would never have known had they not revealed it.

Faoi Ghlas

I wasn't exactly concentrating on the Peeler's faces that night.

In an aggressive and hostile manner, they proceeded to question us as to where we were going and coming from. We gave them the minimum of information and Anne gave them some abuse in return before we were allowed on about our business. I had been somewhat worried as when prisoners are released on parole they are given a form to carry on them at all times explaining their circumstances of release.

I had left mine in my mother's house as I set off for the parade but fortunately the RUC members believed I was out of jail for good and I didn't have to produce the form. In all likelihood they would have returned me to the jail forthwith.

As the summer of 1991 approached I wound down completely. Light, easy to read books were the order of the day. Thoughts of where I would live upon release drifted in and out of my mind more frequently. I did not want to live with my parents. Apart from the fact I was too old there was the issue of security. If Easter was anything to go by I would be a target for harassment by the Brits and RUC and I didn't want to bring that to my parent's house. They had suffered it for long enough.

In June I celebrated my 26th birthday. Some cards reminded me it was to be last inside. I bought a load of Thank You cards and sent them out to people such as Nellie McCaughley, Mary Shannon, My Aunt Ena and Mr. and Mrs. Rooney* - people who had never forgotten me and sent me cards for every occasion. I also sent a card to each of my sisters as a token of my gratitude for their love and support throughout the years.

*Since the first edition of Faoi Ghlas was published, Nellie McCaughley, Mary Shannon and Mr. Rooney have all passed away. Go ndearna Dia Trocaire orthu.

Faoi Ghlas

A few days before my release I was granted an inter wing visit with Sean. I travelled in the blacked out prison van to his wing where we spent a couple of hours together. I also saw Danny Morrison there whom I had last seen while canvassing for Sinn Fein during one of many elections.

Dutch Holland was on our wing at this time and it transpired that he was also to be released on the same day as me. Dutch loved the craic of the Big Pitch and thus, three days before our release, the boys organised a 'testimonial' match.

Those of us who were 26 and under would play those over and above that age. Dutch was about forty!!!! Before the match we were both presented with pennants signed by everyone.

Obviously our team won – I scored two goals in a 2-1 win and to add insult to injury I cleared a certain equalizer off the line from Dutch! Sorry Dutch!

On Thursday 1st August 1991, the day before our release our comrades threw a party for us in H8. At the end we were given presentations as mementos of our time there in the Blocks. I received a portrait of Bobby Sands inscribed with the words:

"They will not criminalise us...rob us of our true identity...steal our individualism...depoliticise us...churn us out as systemised, institusionalised, decent law-abiding robots. Never will they label our liberation struggle as criminal".

Dutch said a few words at the end. I couldn't speak. I was too choked. Dutch felt the same but was composed enough to speak. I remember after his presentation he in turn presented the wing O.C. with his blue

Faoi Ghlas

Long Kesh cup - the cup he had drank out of for years, the one he had carried round with him from block to block!

I slept fairly well that night and wakened early the next morning. Shortly after this our block was called for the football pitch. I was asked did I want to go. Not likely I thought. In a way I was glad the pitch had been called.

There would be less people there as I walked out of the wing and through the gates.

Around 11 o'clock I was called out by the screw and made my way out the wing gate. Tom McAllister waved to me from the other wing and I waved back before walking through the circle to board the mini-bus that would take me to the main prison exit.

The escorting screw was quiet and there was little said between us. At the administration area I was photographed and fingerprinted. The Governor presented me with my release licence and reminded me that if my licence was revoked I could be returned to jail at anytime. I nodded politely, put the licence into my pocket, lifted my bag of belongings and left.

As I was led across the area to the exit - the reverse of my walk in March 1986 - I looked at the sky. This time it was blue and the sun was shining.

Through the turnstile and out of the H-Blocks I walked.

On the other side of the fence was my Mother;

"Welcome Home Son" she said.

Faoi Ghlas

Annie Adams 1924 - 1992

Faoi Ghlas

Faoi Ghlas

Glossary

Page 1. Screws: Prison Officers.
Page 5. Skeet: Peter 'Skeet' Hamilton (Ardoyne) was a life sentence Republican prisoner and a great character who attempted to escape from Long Kesh many times.
Page 9. Chopper: Paddy McCotter (Lenadoon).
Page 9. Hucker: Gerard Moyna (Clonard).
Page 9. Craic/Mixing: Fun and joking.
Page 9. The Army: The Irish Republican Army.
Page 11. O.C. Officer Commanding.
Page 14. Tuso: Tony McCabe (Turf Lodge).
Page 14. Micky Mul: Micky Mulvenna (Ballymurphy).
Page 14. Spud: Martin Murphy (Iveagh).
Page 15. Scéal: Irish for news.
Page 17. Ceannfort: Irish for Officer Commanding.
Page 19. Fitzy: Pat Fitzpatrick (Markets).
Page 23. I.O. Intelligence Officer.
Page 36. Mo Chara: Irish for My Friend.
Page 38. Micky John McVey (Tyrone) Ta Buck :Tommy Bradley (Ardoyne).
Page 43. Dump: The term used to describe an IRA weapons hide.
Page 43. Tic Tac: Micky Culbert (Andersontown).
Page 43. Ginty: Seán Lennon (Andersontown).
Page 46. Big Marshall: Marshall Mooney. (R.I.P.) (Ballymurphy).
Page 46. Duice: John McMullan (R.I.P.) (Ardoyne).
Page 47. Buiochas le Dia: Irish for Thank God.

Faoi Ghlas

Page 48. Axel: Paul Creighton, an innocent man from Ballymurphy was wrongly convicted of Republican activity and served 15 years in prison.

Page 49. Leine Bán: Irish for White Shirt: Senior screws wore white shirts and thus the name given to them.

Page 55. Peelers: Royal Ulster Constabulary,

Page 59. Seosamh Gault: Joe Simpson (Andersontown).

Page 61. Tomboy: Tomboy Loudon (Unity Flats).

Page 61. Digger: Digger McCrory (Turf Lodge).

Page 63. Meaders: Brendy Mead (St James's).

Page 64. Wee Teapot: Ciaran McMullan (Clonard).

Page 64. Big Jazz: Jim McCann (Anderonstown).

Page 70. Tonkas: Tom Moran (Turf Lodge).

Page 70. Spike: Seán Murray (Clonard).

Page 70. Bap: Frank McGreavey (R.I.P.) (Falls Road).

Page 70. Ranganna: Irish for classes.

Page 72. Rinty: Tom McVeigh (Andersontown).

Page 73. Dikel: Michael Gorman (Ardoyne).

Page 73. Pickles: John Pickering (Andersontown).

Faoi Ghlas

Faoi Ghlas

Printed in Great Britain
by Amazon